Michael Moran, CEO of the career coaching consultancy 10Eighty, brings his extensive experience to this guide. As a seasoned career coach, Michael has worked with clients across a range of areas including those seeking new jobs, setting up business and, most recently, building thriving portfolio careers.

10EIGHTY

"

Michael has been my go-to trusted career management advisor for many years, providing professional and practical guidance on career management for both my teams and myself. For those looking to make a transition into portfolio career, this is a must read book providing pragmatic advice and support based on many years of experience, knowledge and research on what it really takes to make a successful transition to a portfolio career, thereby ensuring your dreams become a reality. "

Andrew Clayton, former 10Eighty client and an expert in customer experience ex-BUPA and E.ON

GOing Portfolio

How to build a portfolio career

by
Michael Moran

This book is dedicated to my wife Joan, daughter Hannah and son Tom.

Filament Publishing

Filament Publishing

Published by

Filament Publishing Ltd

14, Croydon Road, Beddington, Croydon, Surrey CR0 4PA

www.filamentpublishing.com

+44 (0)20 8688 2598

Going Portfolio by Michael Moran

ISBN 978-1-915465-68-9

Printed in the UK

Contents

Chapter Ten

Chapter Eleven

Chapter Twelve

Chapter Thirteen

Chapter Fourteen

" Michael didn't just help me find answers — he helped me ask the right questions. "

John Marsland

Foreword

When I left my role at Schroders after sixteen years, I had no idea what lay ahead. It was an exciting yet daunting time. The world of work had shifted, particularly after the pandemic, and like many I found myself reflecting on what I wanted from the next chapter of my career. Would I stay in a corporate environment? Try something entirely different? Or carve out a path that blended my skills, interests and passions?

It was during this period of transition that I met Michael Moran through 10Eighty's career coaching programme. Michael didn't just help me find answers — he helped me ask the right questions. His advice fundamentally changed how I thought about my career, particularly the importance of networking. I'd always been hesitant to lean on my connections but Michael helped me see networking not as a transaction but as a way to unlock opportunities by building genuine relationships.

As you'll discover in this book, making the leap to a portfolio career isn't about having all the answers from day one. It's a journey of exploration — understanding your skills, identifying what drives you and learning how to position yourself to add value in different contexts. Michael's insights, tools and strategies were instrumental in helping me navigate that process.

Today, my portfolio career includes advisory roles, consultancy and a chairmanship as well as involvement in my late father's family business. Each element brings something unique, offering variety, challenge and fulfilment. The balance I've achieved between work and life is something I never thought possible during my corporate years. But, as Michael often reminds his clients, balance isn't something that happens to you — it's something you actively create.

This book is an essential guide for anyone considering a portfolio career, whether you're at the start of your journey or rethinking how to structure your portfolio more effectively. Michael's deep understanding of what it takes to make this transition is clear in every chapter. He brings together practical advice, thought-provoking questions and real-life stories (including mine) to show that a portfolio career isn't just a fallback option; it's a dynamic, rewarding way to work that's increasingly relevant in today's world.

If you're reading this, you've already taken an important first step: exploring what's possible. Let this book be your companion, coach and guide. It's not just a resource, it's a blueprint for creating a career that truly works for you.

I owe a great deal to Michael and his team for helping me find my way. I hope my story — and the many insights in this book — inspire you to take the leap and discover the benefits of going portfolio.

John Marsland

" I first met Michael when we both served as Board members of London HR Connection (LHRC). I was immediately struck by the depth and breadth of experience he brings not only to the HR and People agenda but also to the broader issues inherent in running businesses — so much so that, when the time came for me to seek advice on my commercial options in transforming the business model for LHRC and taking it independent, Michael was the first person whose advice I sought (and subsequently followed, to great effect)

This for me exemplifies the work he does and the strengths he has in coaching and mentoring leaders to develop their own strategies at pivotal points of change, by guiding them through a process of reflection and challenge to take them closer to their personal goals. "

Craig McCoy,
Chair — London HR Connection

Going Portfolio: How to build a portfolio career

Preface

To understand the journey that brings me to this book,
it helps to start with a belief I've held since the beginning:
careers are too important to leave in the hands of others.

While I may not have had a portfolio career in the classic sense, every step of my path has been driven by the same principles that underlie this approach — seeking purpose, making calculated choices and staying open to change. I haven't always known where each decision would take me but I've always trusted in the power of learning, resilience, and connection to move me forward.

My interest in HR began early, inspired by my father's work as a union branch secretary. From an initial fascination with industrial relations my first professional role in HR was with the NHS, where I spent the early part of my career navigating a diverse and complex environment — one where patient care was the priority but funding and resources were often in short supply. I later discovered I was offered the job to ensure the role was not "lost" in a hiring freeze!

My years in the NHS gave me a crash course in people management and the challenges of a highly regulated, politically sensitive workplace. They taught me that great teams need more than just policies; they need leaders who understand and appreciate the human side of business.

After years in HR leadership at hospitals across Manchester and eventually as Head of HR at an NHS Trust in London, I decided to explore the private sector, driven by curiosity and a desire to test myself in a different environment, one which I felt would be more efficient. My move into insurance — a stark departure from the NHS — was eye-opening. Here, profitability was high but people management lagged far behind. In fact, it was in the dark ages with regards to HR practices and I had my worst boss ever. It wasn't a place where I felt I could make a real impact so I shifted again, this time into a commodities and derivatives brokerage. I was responsible for HR across global offices and, for the first time, I had the autonomy to shape the business culture and craft HR strategies that aligned with the fast-paced demands of the financial industry. This experience gave me insight into the international, high-stakes world of finance, and I learned to adapt to different business norms and expectations.

My career took a turn when my then-employer invited me to move from HR into operations management — a chance to lead from the centre, overseeing the 'back office' while managing revenue-generating activities. It was here that I gained hands-on experience in areas beyond HR, like managing IT projects and relocating an entire dealing room. These years shaped my business acumen and taught me the importance of agility and a broad skill set — qualities I now see as critical for anyone pursuing a portfolio career.

Following this role I joined an outplacement business, a decision that marked a shift in my work toward helping others find their footing in the world of career transitions. At the time I didn't fully grasp what outplacement involved but I soon realised it was a space where I could make a real difference. Helping professionals at pivotal points in their careers became a passion and I had the opportunity to grow from Head of Operations to managing director. This role allowed me to blend my business experience with my desire to make a tangible impact on others' lives. It was a fast-paced environment, shaped by market demands, mergers and shifting client needs, but it reinforced my belief in the value of self-management, resilience and adaptability — qualities central to building a fulfilling, independent career.

It was this same drive to shape my own destiny that led me, years later, to co-found 10Eighty, a business built to support individuals and organisations in pursuing meaningful work. From our modest — and profitable — beginnings in 2012, we've now delivered coaching and leadership development in over 60 countries, working with over half a million clients, and we have more than 100 associates across the globe. Alongside the practical aspects of running a business this venture allowed me to engage deeply with the kind of career coaching I love, encouraging clients to consider not just their next job but the broader picture of what they want from work and life.

My journey has been made all the more rewarding by the talented and passionate people I've had the privilege to share it with. And now, some 12 years later, it's time to hand over the reins. One of my founding partners is poised to step into a leadership role, and my daughter, who joined the business during this journey, has proven to be the perfect counterpart for Liz. Staying true to my philosophy of owning your career and planning ahead, the time is right to prepare to step down — but not away.

I have a deep love for career coaching and as long as I remain relevant to the marketplace, I plan to continue this work. Throughout my career I've had the privilege of mentoring emerging professionals and experienced leaders alike, helping them define and pursue their goals. I've been an active member of the Institute of Personnel Management (now CIPD) for over 40 years, chaired Central London's branch and established a mentoring programme that continues to shape HR professionals' careers. I've mentored more than 50 individuals over the years and one of my earliest mentees is now a professor in HR — a point of personal pride. Mentoring, like any meaningful work, is a reciprocal process. It keeps me engaged with new perspectives, challenges me to stay relevant and continually renews my own understanding of what makes for a thriving, purpose-driven career.

As part of my own learning and growth I have sought opportunities to broaden my business experience by serving as a Non-Executive Director (NED). One particularly fulfilling role was mentoring David Marshall, a former employee, as he founded an e-learning business specialising in diversity and inclusion for the education sector. From its inception to its successful sale to a larger software company in 2022, it was immensely satisfying to support David's entrepreneurial journey.

I also served as an NED for a remuneration consultancy. While my tenure there was shorter, it too concluded with a successful acquisition by an insurance company. These experiences offered valuable insights into different business models, particularly how they engaged and utilised NEDs — a practice we've always valued at 10Eighty. Our own board has consistently benefited from the strategic guidance, market intelligence and sound advice of its Non-Executive Directors.

If there's one theme that runs through my career it's a commitment to finding meaning and fulfilment in work. I have always believed that enjoying what you do is essential and the moment I stopped enjoying something I looked for the next challenge. A portfolio career is, in many ways, the ultimate expression of that mindset. It offers the freedom to follow one's interests, to build a network based on authentic connections and to focus on what truly matters. Whether working in the public or private sector, running my own business or mentoring others, I've aimed to stay true to this principle and it's a perspective that I bring to the advice in this book.

Building a portfolio career is not a linear path, nor is it a quick fix. It requires resilience, a willingness to take risks and a commitment to lifelong learning. My journey may not be typical of a portfolio career but it has prepared me to guide those who are ready to embrace this path. Through this book, I hope to share insights and strategies that will help you take control of your career, find work that aligns with your values and build a life that's both fulfilling and financially secure.

So, here's to the journey — one that doesn't necessarily follow a straight line but that takes you towards work you love and a life that's truly your own.

Michael Moran

Founder and CEO, 10Eighty

10 EIGHTY
Making the world of work a better place

"

I've known Michael Moran for many years, as a valued colleague, inspired mentor and warm-hearted friend. In all that time, the unwavering constant in his DNA has been his passion to help others find their best way forward. I can't think of a better person to be writing 'Going Portfolio' — it's packed to the rafters with valuable and practical advice that readers can put into action straight away. Read this book, and, with Michael's guidance, you'll know straight away that you're in very safe hands.

"

Trevor Merriden, Executive and Career Coach, Entrepreneur, Broadcaster, Speaker, Author

Acknowledgements

All authors acknowledge that their book couldn't have been written without the help of.....

I am no different; indeed without Helen Menhenett there would have been no book. She has taken my ideas and transformed them into a book that I hope will help people change their lives for the better. I have worked with Helen for over 15 years and, during that time, she has worked tirelessly to make my stream of consciousness enthusiasm and terrible grammar into documents that make for easy reading. She is a constant source of inspiration, and her research skills are always on hand to provide a fact to support my hypotheses. Hand on heart, without her, there would be no book. Thank you, Helen.

I also need to acknowledge the contribution of Sian Harrington, who ensured the book got finished.

Big thanks to James Mellor for the cartoons.

Thanks to Lacey Cooper for the front cover design and all graphics.

"Michael is the ultimate 'go to' person for career coaching. I have known him for more years than either of us should perhaps admit, both as a repeat corporate client at 10 Eighty and its forerunners and, more latterly, as a colleague and friend. As well as delivering corporate human capital solutions, he has coached me on a 1:1 basis at several pivotal moments of my career, including when I was 'going portfolio'. I have always benefited hugely from his insightful, pragmatic, supportive and challenging approach, all delivered with generosity, unflinching honesty, warmth, empathy and humour. I appreciated his reality checks. This book encapsulates his immense wisdom and knowledge and is a must-read for anyone contemplating 'going portfolio' or already on that path. It contains insights, reality checks and helpful key takeaways, all written in Michael's unique tone of voice. In a nutshell, it's the next best thing to being coached by Michael in person."

Paula Jordan, Owner at Paula Jordan Consulting, Non-Executive Director at 10Eighty, Chair of Board of Trustees at McCarthy Stone Foundation and Member of the Board and Chair of the Remuneration Committee of Sparsholt College Group.

Contributors

10Eighty fields a team of experienced, qualified and professional executive coaches, facilitators and leadership consultants who work with clients to build plans tailored to their organisation and goals. Our coaches are portfolio professionals and alongside their experience as coaches and mentors they work or have worked in professional services, financial services, the public sector, manufacturing, HR and marketing.

Our principles are straightforward:

- Everyone has potential and should have the opportunity to develop and realise that potential.
- We enable individuals to be comfortable and confident in taking ownership and responsibility for their actions and behaviours.
- Allowing everyone to operate independently and interdependently is a core element of our development programmes.
- We promote a strengths-based philosophy to enhance management and leadership capability and increase career resilience.
- The work we do should be of benefit to the individuals, organisations and communities we serve.
- Everything we do, we do with passion.

The 10Eighty executive coaches who contributed to this book provided insights from their own successful portfolio careers and also from their work with our clients; they include:

Carol Ashton, David Bridges, Mike Grant, Chris Hale, Michaela Henshaw, Charles Hindson, Barry Joinson, Jeremy Leadsom, Michele Lahey, David Mellor, Paul Mussenden, Sue Mandelbaum, Mark Sismey-Durrant, Andrew Tallents and Tim Parrack.

We talked to them about their portfolio careers, their motivation and the challenges they faced; we asked what they learned about themselves in the process and for their advice to readers.

" The job for life has been replaced with more fluid and individual career choices. You can work for whom you want, when you want. "

Chapter One

The portfolio revolution:

Designing a career you love and getting paid for it

This book is not for you if you are like my friends, Liz and Kim. Both had good jobs and built successful careers without ever loving what they did. They couldn't wait to retire at the first available opportunity.

This book is for you if...

- You are not in a rush to retire
- You feel you still have more value to offer to work
- You are looking to change the way you work

In the old days, retirement was something we used to look forward to in our late 50s to early 60s, and the usual model was a pipe and slippers or golf course and cruise scenario. Many retirees didn't live long enough to enjoy their pension for more than a few years. Life expectancy at birth in 1930 was only 58 for men and 62 for women, and the retirement age was 65.

Increasingly, people are financially secure earlier in their 50s than used to be the case, and they then have a 20 years or so phase when their professional career is over, but they still want to do something useful and productive with their time.

There are also those who are not financially secure and need to work into their 70s. They may have to step back from a corporate role for one reason or another but can't afford to retire. These people will need to settle on alternative work patterns.

Meanwhile, for younger workers, there are generations coming through who will never have the traditional corporate career of the past and for whom work is insecure and predicated on short-term contractual arrangements.

The good news is that today, more and more of us are self-employed by choice; not because we can't find a permanent job, but because we want a different way of working and living. And we can do this because there's a new employment model in town.

If you have skills that the market requires then you no longer need to tie yourself to one corporate employer. The job for life has been replaced with more fluid and individual career choices. You can work for whom you want, when you want and for multiple clients — what we might characterise as a 'gun for hire' strategy.

You may be part-time, full-time, working for yourself as a consultant, freelance operative or contractor and/or for an organisation or organisations. You can mix this with voluntary or pro-bono projects and the pursuit of personal development. This is the portfolio career.

Those pursuing a portfolio career sell their skills and knowledge directly to several clients, thus creating a 'portfolio' of paid activities. The portfolio professional differs from other independent contractors because they are committed to their portfolio as a long-term career choice, based on specialised expertise and unique identity.

Every new venture has implicit in it the risk of failure, and embarking on a portfolio career is an adventurous, challenging and exciting professional step. My philosophy is that if it doesn't work out, it is not a failure but a learning opportunity.

Making the change to a portfolio way of working is a great opportunity to think hard about what you want from your life and career. That may be some specific short-term change or an overhaul of your whole life. You may have been working in one job or sector for a year, 10 or 30 years but feel you want something different. Many people are disenchanted, disillusioned or disappointed in their careers after a number of years in a role, but it's always possible to make a change.

Take William (not his real name), an equity partner I remember. He is highly successful at a City firm and well regarded. But his client contacts are getting older, moving on and/or taking retirement. His employer wants to retain the corporate clients he handles but to do so using younger associates. The world around our partner has changed and younger, hungrier executives are snapping at his heels. The firm has created a succession plan to seamlessly move the older partner on.

Our experienced professional, however, is not ready for a life on the golf course — and in my experience here is an example where there is a real need for advice. Such professionals have often not planned for this scenario and are ill-prepared for embarking on a portfolio career. They need the help of an experienced career coach to make the transition; help that covers everything from being able to set up a printer at home to putting together a marketing campaign that will win new clients.

I absolutely believe it is possible to make the transition from corporate life to portfolio career. However, most people need help with the transition. That is the objective of this book.

In the following chapters, we'll embark on a transformative journey together. You'll learn how to identify your unique blend of skills and passions and strategically assemble them into a thriving, multifaceted career. You'll discover how to build your network, create and demonstrate your personal brand and balance the competing demands that 'going portfolio' creates. You'll hear from those in different stages of their portfolio journey and learn from their lessons.

While this book is mainly aimed at those at a late stage along the career pathway — those at a level where they are thinking of leaving behind their professional career to do other things — we also look at how to embrace a portfolio career at a young age. Portfolio is not just for pensioners!

Part of the attraction of the portfolio route is the opportunity to balance 'work' with other interests. Professionals may plan to take the portfolio option when they reach a certain age and build experience and garner networking contacts with that in mind.

For others, the pathway is less well delineated and planning is ad hoc. Among our interviewees and wider acquaintances many took the portfolio route because they had been made redundant or expected to be let go. Others made a conscious decision to change their way of life. Some made the change due to health issues or family responsibilities.

Other colleagues balance paid work with other responsibilities or with sport, leisure, study or hobby activities, and, for some, those other interests came to constitute a 'side hustle'. Whatever the reason, while the portfolio pathway is not for the faint-hearted, for the majority the benefits outweigh the risks.

So, are you yearning for more than the traditional 9-to-5 grind? Do you crave variety, flexibility and the freedom to pursue your passions? Can you imagine a world where Mondays ignite excitement instead of dread, where your work aligns with your values and interests and where your income streams are as varied as your talents? That world is entirely within reach. Welcome to the portfolio career.

Journey to a portfolio career:
Lessons from John Marsland

John Marsland spent 16 successful years at Schroders in a senior role, leaving on good terms and ready for a change. Today, he thrives in a portfolio career, balancing multiple roles: non-executive director and chair at Strata, advisor to two fintech start-ups, consultant for an investment platform and a guiding hand in his late father's gas engineering business.

During a period of gardening leave, John was offered career coaching through 10Eighty and was introduced to Michael Moran. Open-minded about his next step,s he quickly realised his CV needed updating and began exploring options. A pivotal conversation about networking reshaped his approach. Though initially hesitant to ask friends or acquaintances for help, John took Michael's advice: the right opportunities would come from his network, not traditional applications.

This shift in mindset proved transformative. John began strategically reconnecting with his network, catching up with people he hadn't spoken to in years. While he had no immediate agenda, these conversations helped him reflect on what he truly wanted — whether to return to corporate life or pursue something different.

A Turning Point

The pandemic had changed corporate culture and John realised he no longer wanted a traditional role. His entrepreneurial spirit, which thrived in Schroders' intrapreneurial environment, sought a new outlet.

The passing of his father became a tipping point. Taking on responsibilities in the family business not only gave him purpose but also clarity: it was the perfect time to step away from corporate life and explore something more varied and balanced.

With Michael's help, John began evaluating his options. Was he looking for one major venture or several smaller ones? The idea of managing multiple roles appealed to him but he was mindful of maintaining a healthier work-life balance. Years of work-related travel had strained family life and he was ready for change.

The Portfolio Career

John discovered that defining his value was central to building a portfolio career. In a corporate role, context often frames your contributions, but in this new landscape he had to clearly articulate how his skills and experience added value to others.

By investing in his network, John unlocked unexpected opportunities. Through conversations and new connections he found roles that suited his strengths and interests. Companies looking for expertise — particularly smaller, fast-growing ones — were eager for his insights. Today, his portfolio career seamlessly combines consultancy, advisory work and directorships.

Advice and Reflections

Looking back, John wishes he'd started networking earlier. The connections he made not only led to opportunities but also offered him a renewed sense of purpose. "You need to think hard about what you enjoy and how you can create value for others," he says.

For John, every element of his portfolio career brings something unique. His work with the family business is particularly fulfilling, allowing him to contribute to its legacy — especially its commitment to apprenticeships and developing young talent. Many portfolio professionals find an anchor and for John this is it.

John now enjoys a better work-life balance. While a portfolio career can have its ups and downs, it offers control and flexibility. He's prioritised his health, spends more time with family and takes time for himself — all while engaging in work that excites and challenges him.

His journey stands as a testament to the power of embracing change, building connections and finding purpose in a career that's truly your own.

Chapter Two

A tapestry of talents:
Unpacking the portfolio career

Picture this: a seasoned professional engrossed in a diverse world of strategic boardroom decisions, charitable impact, fly fishing adventures and invigorating nature walks. A life that stretches far beyond a 12-year tenure as an infantry officer in the British Army and two subsequent decades scaling the corporate ladder in asset management. Welcome to Jeremy Leadsom's portfolio life.

Jeremy was highly successful in a corporate career that mainly took in sales and marketing roles. But he envisioned a life with purpose beyond his full-time job. He knew he wanted to do other things while he still had excess energy. He wanted to work part-time, to be busier in the winter in order to release time to do other things in the summer, and to do some unpaid work. So, in the past three years he has been building a portfolio career.

Jeremy planned for the transition by informing his employer three years in advance to facilitate succession planning. He knew what he wanted to do but was not entirely sure how to execute it, so sought advice from friends. His circle was divided: half told him to switch off and do something completely different, but he knew that was not right for him.

In Jeremy's world, it's not merely about working differently — it's about working purposefully. For him, the joy isn't just in the variety — it's in the tangible value he brings to each endeavour.

> *"The variety is great when you have a portfolio career. You have a range of things on the go. What makes it fun and worthwhile is if I can add value, and can see it."*

And there lies his sweet spot — using his skills and expertise to drive organisations forward, especially when he can witness the profound impact of his contributions, such as assisting a charity to diversify its income stream by effectively pitching to potential investors. Giving back like this can be a pillar of a fulfilling portfolio career.

So, what exactly is a portfolio career? At its core, a portfolio career is a kaleidoscope of professional endeavours. It's akin to juggling several part-time jobs concurrently, each reflecting different facets of your skills and interests. It can include activities unrelated to previous experience, perhaps something you've long wanted to turn your hand to, such as pro bono services, volunteering or learning. It's about using the skills you have at your disposal to make a freelance living, and doing it in a way that's rewarding and provides you with choice and variety.

My concept of the ideal portfolio career involves a revenue-generating stream alongside an element of putting back into society/community, such as trustee roles and volunteering and making time for yourself and other priorities. Portfolio working means you have control over how you split your time between work, home and leisure.

A well-designed portfolio is a collection of activities that fit together to form a balanced whole. Your portfolio career might comprise a combination of elements that suit your interests and aspirations, including but not confined to:

- One or more paid part-time or job share roles
- Freelance, contract, interim or temporary roles
- Running a business on a self-employed basis, either exploiting your established professional expertise or tackling something new
- Non-executive directorship or trustee roles
- Coaching, mentoring or training others
- Pro-bono services for organisations or individuals
- Charity or volunteering roles
- Leisure or sport activities
- Creative activities, possibly for payment or just for fun
- Learning on a formal or informal basis either for professional or personal development
- Travel and exploration
- Caring and family responsibilities

Harvard Business School's Christina Wallace sums up this approach as having a 'portfolio life'. In her book 'The Portfolio Life', she talks about an anti-hustle, pro-rest approach to work-life balance built on three tenets:

1. You are more than any one role or opportunity
2. Diversification will help you navigate change and mitigate uncertainty
3. When (not if) your needs change, you can and should rebalance

It's no surprise that the idea of a portfolio career has gained more traction in recent years when you consider the changes in work and life (for more on this, see below and Chapter 3).

However, the word portfolio itself has been around for centuries. Coming from porta, imperative of portare 'to carry' and foglio 'sheet, leaf', from Latin folium (folio), a portfolio is used to mean:

- A collection of drawings, designs, or other papers that represent a person's work
- Or, a collection of different investments that are owned by a particular person or organisation
- Or, the range of products or services that a company offers or the businesses that someone owns

We first hear about the word portfolio being attached to careers in author and philosopher Charles Handy's 1989 management classic, 'The Age of Unreason'. In this book, he uses the phrase 'portfolio life' to refer to the reorganisation of careers as portfolios full of different jobs. Handy was, no doubt, ahead of his time, but I am certain he was right. Portfolio careers for those in their 50s and 60s will be the new norm.

In fact, Handy doesn't see portfolio working as just a trend but as the whole future of work. His book 'The Elephant and the Flea' envisages the future worker as a self-employed independent, hopping between elephantine corporations. These big companies, he suggests, will become places where knowledge workers serve their apprenticeships before leaving, or being ejected, into a world in which they will forge their own way.

Others have made similar predictions. Mirvis and Hall's (1994) 'boundaryless career' and Peiperl and Baruch's (1997) 'post-corporate career' are all models that suggest many are now more flexible in their approach to work, willing to move between a number of different organisations to carry out their work and having a variety of jobs across their careers.

It's not a new concept. For a long time, it's the way most people worked in order to make ends meet. But with industrialisation, more workers were able to pursue specific and specialised roles and came to expect long-term jobs in the sector of their choice. The norm in the workplace until quite recently was that we worked for one or two employers for our whole career, retiring with a gold watch or carriage clock and a pension at 60 or 65. It used to be that we expected to move through a series of roles, working upwards through the hierarchy until retirement. That way of working has, more or less, now disappeared.

The way we find jobs and the way we plan our careers is different for workers in the 2020s than for those who started work in the 1970s and 1980s; more so than I could have imagined in 1976 when I secured my first proper job as a higher clerical officer in the NHS. A career can no longer be characterised as an upward progress through the organisational or occupational hierarchy. This is exemplified by the more adaptive model emerging which Cathy Benko, vice chairman and managing principal at Deloitte, dubbed the 'corporate lattice'. A lattice is a multi-dimensional structure that extends infinitely in any direction; an adaptive construct chock full of options:

- **Careers** today rarely follow a straight line, zig-zagging rather taking a linear path. In their book, 'The Squiggly Career', Helen Tupper and Sarah Ellis highlight how, instead of climbing a predictable ladder, professionals often navigate this lattice — moving sideways, upwards or even downwards to explore new opportunities and develop diverse skills. This shift reflects the increasing complexity and dynamism of the modern workplace, where adaptability and continuous learning are essential. A squiggly career embraces this fluidity. It allows individuals to redefine success on their own terms, blending roles that align with their passions, values and strengths.

  The squiggly career thrives in organisations that foster growth through lattices rather than ladders: those that provide platforms for employees to experiment, learn and grow beyond traditional boundaries. For individuals, it's about embracing self-awareness, creating meaningful networks and continually developing transferable skills. With this approach, professionals can chart careers that are both purpose-driven and adaptable to the ever-changing world of work. Lattice organisations offer more flexible options for growing and a multitude of opportunities to develop.

- **Work** is now about where you go to do what you do rather than expecting people to sit at their desks clocking facetime from 9 to 5. Lattice organisations offer options for when, where and how people do their work.

- **Participation** is top down and all in, where instead of static top-down communications lattice organisations nurture transparent cultures, providing multiple ways for their people to offer thoughts, ideas and feedback.

  More of us work under alternative forms of contract which are often different from traditional 'work'. They transform the traditional one-to-one relationship between employer and employee and are characterised by unconventional work patterns and places of work. It is no longer a case of employed or self-employed, full time or part time. Freelance, contractor, temporary and contingent contracts are now common whether part time or full time.

  Casual work, where the employment is not stable and continuous and the employer is not obliged to regularly provide the worker with work but has the flexibility of calling them in on demand, is normalised in the zero hours contract. New forms of contract and model have emerged in the so-called gig economy:

  - Employee sharing: where a group of employers hires workers and is jointly responsible for them. The concept is similar to temporary agency work, with the purpose of sharing staff to balance the human resources needs of companies while providing secure employment to workers and where the organisations providing the workers does not aim to make a profit.

- Job sharing: where an employer hires several workers to jointly fill a single full-time position. It's a form of part-time work, the purpose of which is to ensure that the shared job is permanently staffed.

- Interim management: where an agency 'leases out' workers to other companies temporarily and for a specific purpose. Unlike temporary agency work, these staff tend to be highly specialised experts who are sent to the receiving companies to solve a specific management or technical challenge or to assist in economically difficult times. Interim management has some elements of consultancy but the expert has the status of an employee rather than of an external advisor. In practice, however, interim management is undertaken on the basis of self-employment in many countries.

- ICT-based mobile work: where the employee or self-employed worker operates from various possible locations outside the premises of their employer (for example, at home, at a client's premises or 'on the road'), supported by modern technologies such as laptop and tablet computers. It is less 'place-bound' than traditional teleworking

- Platform work: where supply and demand for paid labour is matched through an online platform or an app. Employment status is almost always self-employed or freelance. In essence, this is the Uber model of employment.

- Portfolio work: where there is small-scale contracting by freelancers, the self-employed or micro enterprises who work for a large number of clients.

- Collaborative employment: where specific forms of cooperation or networking among the self-employed go beyond traditional supply chain or business partner relationships.

[Adapted from Eurofound research report New Forms of Employment, 2020 update]

In practice, a specific employment relationship can fall into more than one of the above categories (for example, platform workers tend to be portfolio workers).

Reasons for choosing portfolio working

For many, disillusionment with corporate life and career progression, changing values and wellbeing issues are likely to influence the choice of some form of portfolio work as a strong option given their professional and personal circumstances. Self-employment and portfolio careers offer workers a pathway to independence, enable them to be in charge of their own destiny and have more meaning. Italian economist Paolo Verme, of the World Bank, says:

"Freedom is by far the most significant predictor of life satisfaction".

Portfolio workers value the freedom, meaning and control that comes with self-employment; 85% of micro-business owners report they are "more creative, autonomous and satisfied in their work".

The most common reasons I have seen for people choosing portfolio work are listed below:

- You have different skills and interests that you want to use and explore
- A portfolio career helps you design and create your work life to suit you and your aspirations
- You are actively seeking more variety and choice
- You are seeking meaning and purpose, and a portfolio career enables you to earn money and give back
- You want to be your own boss, making decisions and taking action based upon your own judgement and being responsible for the development of your career
- You value autonomy and the high level of self-management involved in this kind of work provides that. You want to be responsible for the success or failure of all work carried out and the ultimate success or failure of your career.

Whatever your reasons for choosing a portfolio career, it's important to realise that it may take time to achieve the balance that suits you best and that there may be compromises and trade-offs to be made. You are likely to have to balance autonomy against uncertainty. You may feel, for instance, that you are trading a measure of financial security for greater freedom or variety.

What is clear, though, is that today we are more likely to gravitate from a full-time job to a portfolio career. We'll hope to work when we want to, probably not for a single employer but on a consultancy, freelance or contract basis — with time to do other things that interest us. Whether that's consulting based on your prior experience, diving into volunteer work that warms your heart or exploring a long-held passion, a portfolio career is about curating a livelihood as unique as you are. In the next chapter we will look at why now is a great time to start your portfolio career.

Key Takeaways

1. Every portfolio career is unique: No two paths look the same — your journey is yours to shape.

2. Portfolio careers are on the rise: More people are embracing this flexible and fulfilling way of working.

3. It's about pursuing what matters to you: At its core, portfolio working is about doing what you love and finding purpose in your work.

Chapter Three

Seizing the moment:
Why a portfolio career is today's ultimate employability strategy

We're in a new era of work. One where your unique blend of skills, knowledge, understanding and personal attributes is the hottest currency in the marketplace. Today, employability is the name of the game.

Employability isn't just about landing a job; it is about a broader set of skills and attributes that enable a successful career and working life.

In this unpredictable age, as Reid Hoffman, author of 'The Alliance: Managing Talent in the Networked Age', aptly notes, the guarantee of lifelong employment feels like an artefact from a bygone era. The old model of guaranteed long-term employment no longer works in a business environment defined by continuous change.

Today, the spotlight is on the flexible, the creative, the active; those who don't just adapt to change but who thrive when they're on a specific 'tour of duty,' when they have a mission that's mutually beneficial to employee and company that can be completed in a realistic period of time.

In my previous book, 'The Guide to Everlasting Employability', I quoted hockey legend Wayne Gretzky: "I skate to where the puck is going to be, not to where it has been." When we understand and identify forward-looking trends, when we are in tune with the marketplace, then we are able to be proactive in managing our careers; by skating to where the puck is going to be.

Our world has shifted in seismic ways, thanks in part to the changing nature of business and the rise of the knowledge worker, changed contracts of employment and an economic landscape where financial and job security are no longer guaranteed. The COVID-19 pandemic only accelerated this transformation. Malcolm Gladwell, author of 'The Tipping Point', talks about

"the moment of critical mass, the threshold, the boiling point"

at which things suddenly and drastically change. COVID-19 has proved to be a tipping point in respect to where and how we work. Our workspaces extended into our homes, commutes turned into walks down the hallway and the traditional 9 to 5 workday was rewritten.

No longer tethered to the office, armed with high-speed broadband and empowered by tools like Zoom and Microsoft Teams, a world of work that catered to our strengths, passions and lifestyle was no longer just a pipe dream. The boom in flexible office spaces and co-working hubs further fuels this fire, creating a landscape ripe for freelancers and portfolio professionals to not just survive but thrive. Working from home is not possible for everyone, and some actively miss the workplace, but I suspect there is no going back. And we can expect that one of the unexpected consequences of the pandemic will be growth in the popularity of the portfolio career.

So let's delve into three reasons why now is the moment to embrace the portfolio career.

Shift in employment patterns and preferences
Changing nature of jobs

At one time, good workers traditionally had a 'job for life' in a single company. Now most professionals work in a number of different job roles until they reach retirement age, sometimes changing career too. To illustrate this, let's take pensions. The basis on which company pensions were established was predicated on a 40 years' service record, with a pension based on 80th or 60th accruals, if you were lucky. My father's career advice was to get a job with a secure employer — he worked all his life for British Rail and could not have envisaged a career which entailed working for between five to 10 different employers.

The advent of the money purchase pension reflects the fact that the employer for life model is dead in the water. Many employers have taken the view, rightly or wrongly, that all that matters is shareholder value, and consequently they have no loyalty to employees. The important thing is ensuring that costs are minimised and margin is maximised. Perhaps I may be overstating the case, but there is no doubt the 'one employer for life' model is long gone.

While standard employment (permanent, full-time employment based on labour law) remains dominant, the workplace is characterised by an increasing diversity of employment forms. The gig economy, with its non-traditional work arrangements, reflects this trend as companies use independent contractors and make full-time permanent roles into several part-time jobs. The simple truth is that from the point of view of management it is cheaper to use contractors, freelance and temporary workers.

Desire for flexibility

Today's workforce seeks a different way of working and living, preferring fluid and individual career choices over a fixed career path. Increasingly, people find that they don't want to do the same thing day in and day out. The COVID-19 pandemic made many people reassess their lives and the part that work plays.

Frederick Taylor's scientific management may have been good for productivity and profitability but it did little for job satisfaction and job security. These two competing ideas are leading to a dramatic reappraisal of how we manage our career. We are more used to choice and change as the internet, social media and globalisation are exposing us to new ideas and new perspectives. We like the idea that we can design and change our career as we want.

Furthermore, the gig-economy means we need to be ready to learn new skills as we work, and to watch the market for opportunities and new developments. A 'mix-and-match' approach is appealing to those who want to take control of their work, focus on what they love and achieve good work-life balance. Choosing whom you work with is a big draw for many. If office politics wear you down then the chance to pick and choose your contracts is attractive.

And it's not just employees who want flexibility: employers do too. They want a just in time approach to people — 'I want it now and I want it ready to plug in'. Consequently, when an employee reaches the end of their usefulness, the employer wants to be able to dispense with them with a minimum of fuss. That's not a negative, however. There are benefits for employees when they are able to choose when they want to work, who they want to work for and where.

Technological advancement and globalisation
Digitisation and the 'new normal'

The impact of COVID-19 showcased how the widespread use of digital technologies was crucial in keeping businesses, the workforce and society afloat during the worst of lockdown and the health crisis in 2020. Digitally enabled employment and also those that facilitate the balancing of supply and demand for the workforce (such as employee sharing) are increasingly important as we recover equilibrium and rebuild the economy.

Automation

Technological progress is continuing apace and more employees are finding themselves replaced by robots, software and artificial intelligence. Whole layers of management are being cut back to save money in line with an overall lean trend in business. Technological and economic disruption in many markets and professions is resulting in a lot of redundancies and it is wise to be alive to the changes in the workplace and the options available. Upskilling, reskilling, unlearning and lifelong learning are the name of the game if you are to keep your skills relevant and yourself employable in an automation-charged work environment.

Global and outsourced job market

The job market has become global, hyper-competitive and tech-driven, emphasising contractors over traditional employees. Many employers seek to reduce costs by sending jobs overseas to countries with cheaper labour or to outsource to freelancers.

Changing perspectives on career longevity and retirement

Increased life expectancy and productive work

There's a shift in understanding that professionals can remain productive far beyond traditional retirement age. This is underscored by the idea presented in the book 'The 100-Year Life' by London Business School professors Lynda Gratton and Andrew Scott. They argue that our life stages will have to be reinvented in their book, which looks at the likelihood of living for 100 years and working productively for a greater part of that time.

It's a far cry from the prevailing opinion not that long ago that by age 55 most professionals had peaked and needed to move aside for the next generation. In an era of hard manual work then, yes by 55 a worker may have been physically worn out, but not today in the era of the knowledge worker. The old adage was you can't teach an old dog new tricks, but try telling that to the silver surfer.

The background to this is that life expectancy is rising. Most of us will live into our 80s and beyond, and we don't want to stop working completely at 55 or 60 or 65. Indeed, some can't afford to do so. If we are working towards retirement age and have the cushion of sufficient or alternative incomes from savings, pensions or investments, this significantly reduces the uncertainty resulting from a change of career direction. Also, for those who have enjoyed a successful career, the impact of uncertainty is less pressing when we want to explore new avenues and pastures.

Our ageing population also means increasing numbers of working adults may need to work around family responsibilities, such as caring for frail parents. A portfolio career enables them to do this more easily than full-time employment typically allows.

Rise in self-employment

As we have seen, for most of the 20th century the norm was that once a person embarked on a chosen career path then that was it. You worked hard and moved up the career ladder or corporate hierarchy to the limits of your ambition and talent. But as a result of the trends outlined above, self-employment is growing. Self-employment in professional occupations has risen by 37%, the highest rise of all types of occupation. The number of people who work for themselves but do fewer than 30 hours a week has grown by nearly 65% from 2000, compared with 20% growth in the number of full-time self-employed.

Our experts say:

> Helen Menhenett: *I was unhappy at work but when, at the suggestion of my husband, I thought about making a change, it quickly became obvious that a mix of freelance work and completing my studies was a serious option. I could afford to do it and was pretty sure I could get enough work to keep me as busy as I wanted to be. I juggle freelance work with study and eldercare and have never regretted it.*

David Bridges: **Honestly, I was a little bored of just doing the one thing and wanted a more peripatetic way of working as well as the variety involved in portfolio career. I also felt that for a number of years I had been in a situation where I was doing so much but was not doing any of it well enough, and I wanted more from my working life than that.**

Portfolio working is an approach that we at 10Eighty have cheerfully embraced. We urge clients to strive not for security of employment but for employability; to develop their human capital by taking responsibility for the development and exercise of their skills and strengths.

Smart employees have come to realise, that in the modern workplace, what really matters is employability. Do I have the skills and knowledge the marketplace is demanding? If I have the skills to meet the demands of the market, I can then sell those skills to the highest bidder. In effect the employee is CEO of their career and is self-sufficient and proactive about managing a career pathway that meets their needs and aspirations.

There are benefits and risks, as you will see from the following chapters. But in reality, this more flexible way of working can make you more secure. For those pursuing a portfolio career out of economic necessity I'd cite marketing expert Dorie Clark, professor at Duke University's Fuqua School of Business, who argues it's the best way to hedge against financial risk.

I believe this new employment model is to be welcomed. It affords us a win-win scenario. Employers can pick up and release labour to meet the needs of their business. As a quid pro quo the portfolio careerist has choices, as to for whom, where and when they work. It has to be acknowledged that it's not suitable for everyone and it is dependent on the individual taking responsibility for their career and employability. But if you have the skills and knowledge the marketplace requires, you are the king of your castle.

Key Takeaways

Great news — the timing has never been better: Shifting employer attitudes, high demand for specialised skills, technological advancements and longer lifespans make launching a portfolio career easier than ever.

Understanding yourself — not just as a professional, but as a human being — is key

Chapter Four

Crafting your unique blend:

Unearthing skills, passions and interests for your portfolio journey

So, you've caught the allure of the portfolio career — bravo! But where to begin on this exciting journey? It's time for an honest heart-to-heart with yourself. Before you invest a single penny or a minute of your time, think about why you might want to make such a change.

Ask yourself the following questions:

- What is important to you?
- What are your values?
- What energises you?
- What are you good at?
- What do you offer a prospective client?

KING OF THE CASTLE

Understanding yourself — not just as a professional, but as a human being — is key to your portfolio journey. It's about knowing what you bring to the table and identifying the unique blend of skills and passions that set you apart.

I recommend you think in terms of the intelligent career framework, which suggests careers depend on three interdependent 'ways of knowing' — reflecting why you work (values), how you prefer to work (motivated talents) and with whom you like to work.

By considering your core values, you will achieve a better grasp for what makes you tick. Ask yourself: what values are most useful to me at this time in my life to enable me to get where I want to go? This is step one on your journey to a portfolio career, highlighted at the bottom of the triangle in the visual below.

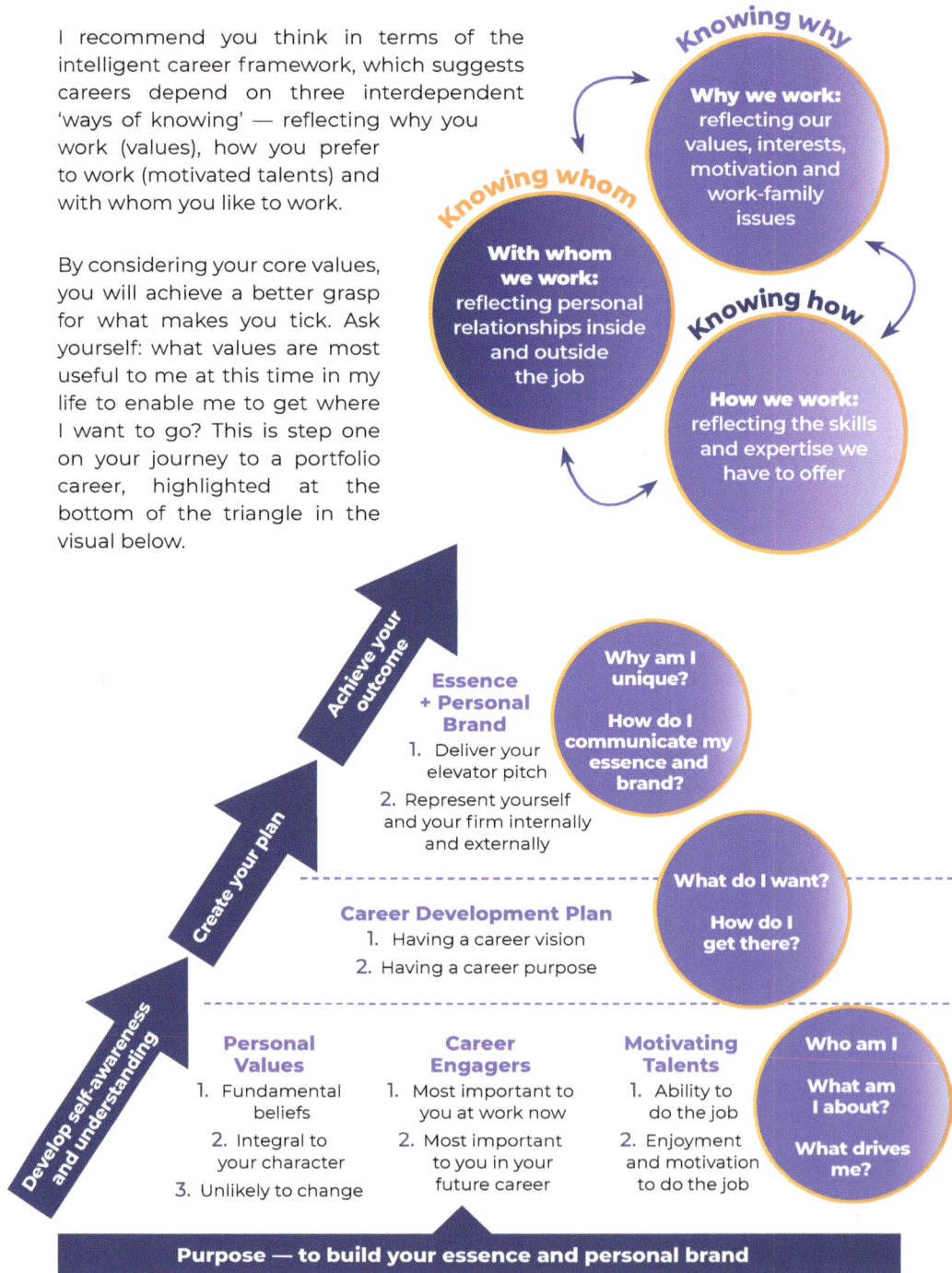

Knowing why

Why we work: reflecting our values, interests, motivation and work-family issues

Knowing whom

With whom we work: reflecting personal relationships inside and outside the job

Knowing how

How we work: reflecting the skills and expertise we have to offer

Achieve your outcome

Create your plan

Develop self-awareness and understanding

Essence + Personal Brand
1. Deliver your elevator pitch
2. Represent yourself and your firm internally and externally

Why am I unique?

How do I communicate my essence and brand?

Career Development Plan
1. Having a career vision
2. Having a career purpose

What do I want?

How do I get there?

Personal Values
1. Fundamental beliefs
2. Integral to your character
3. Unlikely to change

Career Engagers
1. Most important to you at work now
2. Most important to you in your future career

Motivating Talents
1. Ability to do the job
2. Enjoyment and motivation to do the job

Who am I

What am I about?

What drives me?

Purpose — to build your essence and personal brand

So let's look at how to develop this self-awareness and understanding.

Identifying what you value

What do I mean by this? These are the things that are very important to you. In a work/career setting, it is what you want from your chosen job/vocation. The things that motivate you. How you derive job satisfaction.

In the first instance, write down these values in no particular order by committing them to paper. Think about when you were most happy in a work setting. Why was that? What were you doing? Where were you doing it and with whom? Take these values and then mark them with the following letters:

A. Absolutely a fundamental value of mine
B. Nice to have value or a subset of an A value
C. Not relevant to me

Next take your 'A's and rank them 1-5. These are your most important values so list them with number one being your most important value.

The final step is to put into words why each of these values is important to you. Remember, the list can change at any time and is relevant to now and the changes that you are looking for in your life in embarking on a portfolio career.

Overleaf are some values to help you start thinking about this. This list is not comprehensive so add values that seem relevant to you.

Values

Tick one circle if this value is a priority for you and number the other in order of priority.

4 ♦
Having Status
Having position, rank or standing within the organisation
◯ ◯

10 ♥
Relationship Building
Initiate, develop and maintain relationships for mutual benefit
◯ ◯

8 ♣
Celebrating Success
Recognise and reward accomplishment and share good news
◯ ◯

10 ♣
Managing and Supervising Others
Plan, oversee, control and direct the work of staff members
◯ ◯

K ♦
Task Completion
Accomplishing work to expected standards/ requirements
◯ ◯

Q ♥
Preferring clear directions and targets
Accountability for deadlines, budgets and scope of responsibility
◯ ◯

3 ♠
Sense of Belonging
Being part of the team and organisation
◯ ◯

Risk Assessment
Identify, evaluate and estimate levels of risks involved in a situation
◯ ◯

Stretch and Challenge
The opportunity to test and demonstrate the full extent of my knowledge and skills
◯ ◯

10 ♣

Opportunities to Develop Skills

To add value for the employer and my career developments

8 ♠

Power and Control

Control or command over others; authority to exercise power

Personal Growth

To help me in seeking professional and personal excellence

2 ♠

Flexible Working

With flexible hours and location to suit my needs

Ability to work at my own pace

Control and autonomy over the planning and completion of my work

9 ♣

Delivery Against Targets

Meeting performance measurement standards and work requirements

A ♣

Work as Generalist or Specialist

with broad general knowledge, skills and responsibilities in several areas, or strong skills in a distinct area.

7 ♥

Knowing what is expected of me

With clear, reasonable and agreed tasks, standards and objectives

J ♦

Travel as part of my role

Working in more than one location or work-site

From Fuel50: an AI-driven talent marketplace platform that fuels internal talent mobility, workforce agility, employee engagement, talent retention and bottom-line impact within leading organisations all over the world. The platform helps clients create career pathways and journeys within their organisation that match to the wants and needs of their people.

Identify your passions and motivated talents

There's an assumption that once we've chosen our profession or speciality, that's all we want to — or should — do. However, the portfolio career is the chance to extend your reach. There are no rules saying you must have a portfolio composed entirely around your professional qualification.

Passion is the key to developing in any profession but is especially important in a portfolio career. If you want to develop a career in non-executive roles, governance, not-for-profit or a similar field, you need passion and enthusiasm for the work that you are undertaking. That passion is what will enable you to cope with challenges, setbacks, deadlines and a lot of work that you would not ordinarily face in a traditional role. You need all the support that you can get when you don't have a company behind you and you are the face of your brand!

So, think about what elements of your life fill you with joy and enthusiasm? What caters to your passion? What provides satisfaction and fulfilment? You may always have relied on being logical and pursuing fact-based work, but by allowing your creative side to flourish, you may increase wellbeing as well as expanding your horizons.

Make a list of the things you enjoy doing. What do you spend time on? Do not restrict yourself to purely work activities. For example, spending time doing crossword puzzles can also provide a valuable clue to specific skills you have. The key is to identify motivated talents, not just things you do well, but those activities you truly enjoy.

The old adage applies here: find a job you love and you will never work again. The key to a successful portfolio career is to spend your time doing the things you love.

The simple exercise opposite will help you identify your passions and suggest interests you may wish to explore further.

As a result of buying this book you are being given access to 10Eighty's Fuel50 online platform. Email info@10Eighty quoting the code PORTFOLIOCAREER to gain access to three questionnaires, personal values, career engagers and motivated talents. The latter is help you identify your key skills. Fuel50 is an AI-driven talent marketplace platform that fuels internal talent mobility, workforce agility, employee engagement, talent retention and bottom-line impact within leading organisations all over the world. The platform helps clients create career pathways and journeys within their organisation that match to the wants and needs of their people. You can find out more in the Appendix One.

Discover Your
Passions Questionnaire

Section 1: Self-Reflection

1. What activities make you lose track of time?

2. What topics do you find yourself reading or learning about most often?

3. When were you last truly excited about something? What was it?

4. Describe a moment when you felt proud of yourself. What were you doing?

5. What are some of your favourite childhood memories? What activities were you engaged in?

Section 2: Interests and Hobbies

6. Which of the following activities do you enjoy? (Select all that apply)

Reading ◯   Cooking or baking ◯   Music (playing/ ◯
Writing ◯   Traveling ◯   listening)
Art and craft ◯ Gardening ◯   Other: *[Please specify]*
Sports and fitness ◯ Volunteering ◯

7. If you could dedicate a day to any hobby, what would you choose?

8. What would you do on a perfect weekend?

What next?

- Review your responses
- Identify patterns, themes and any insights that you may have.

What we know:

Barry Joinson says:

"Fundamental to making a change was the feeling I no longer added value, yet really wanted to make a positive impact. However, finding my purpose was challenging; while I had a sense of what I wanted to do, I didn't know how to articulate it."

Identify your skills

When you embark on your portfolio career, you need to identify sustainable market opportunities. Where does your professional value reside? Understanding the skills you have now and the gaps to the skills you will need for the future is imperative.

- Identify and differentiate what makes you stand out from other professionals. What makes you special and different? What is your unique selling point?
- What are the skills, experience and career mission that characterise your offering?

Work is becoming more hybrid and complex, and demands specific skills, which are multi-disciplinary, often blending left brain (logical, organised) and right brain (creative, artistic).

The core soft skills used at work include:

- Literacy and numeracy
- Time management and organisation
- Adaptability
- Oral and written communication skills
- Creative problem-solving
- Initiative and enterprise
- Critical and analytical thinking
- Information gathering, evaluation and synthesis
- Emotional intelligence and interpersonal skills

Personal attributes such as patience, initiative and empathy are relevant to the type of work that is most likely to suit you. The higher your level of self-awareness, the more likely you are to build a career that fulfils you, because your personality affects your way of working and the way you respond to situations.

You have valuable knowledge, understanding and skills from all your varied experiences, and this includes extracurricular learning, training courses, hobbies, interests and voluntary work. If you haven't been in formal employment for a while, think about the other skills you've developed.

Think about your behaviour, emotions and reactions. Check with people close to you; they may be able to help you identify strengths and qualities that you haven't considered.

Our experts say:

> **Tim Parrack:** *You've got to be the right kind of individual. If you rely on a heavy line of support, you are probably better off in a corporate environment. If you have a natural skill set that includes a consultative attitude to things and being a good influencer, this could be for you. It doesn't suit everyone. To be effective you have to put in some hard graft in terms of developing business.*

Map your skills against those required in the market

The skills most in demand, in business at any rate, are technology skills and soft skills. People who work with data and use technology effectively while also demonstrating the emotional intelligence to collaborate with teams and navigate in a complex, fast-moving and volatile environment have a competitive advantage.

It is important to stress that technical expertise alone will not be sufficient. Soft skills ultimately determine whether you can secure new business and build a successful enterprise. Clients give you more business because they like you; likeability is an essential character trait.

Success in a portfolio career is predicated on being able to manage yourself, your workload and your new business. This takes a blend of skills and attributes, such as:

- The ability to manage a varied workload
- Taking responsibility for your own work, time and energy
- Being well organised
- Clarity about what you can do and what you deserve to be paid
- Confidence to network, seek out work and promote yourself
- Resilience and the ability to recover from setbacks quickly

For a portfolio to be a serious option, you need a range of skills that are transferable. Think about your natural market — pursuing the profession for which you trained but also consider taking those skills and seeing how they transfer to other sectors. So, if you were selling in the financial services space, could you sell your services to financial services? If you worked in the not for profit sector stay with causes you care about but look at new routes and lines of business.

Key skills

I suggest you do the exercise overleaf to help you identify the skills that will be most applicable to your portfolio. When you have done this, it's important to think about skills you don't have but may need in the future to meet your aspirations and to ensure a sustainable long-term career path. Then plan to acquire those skills and put them to use (you can find out more about this in the next chapter). Find the top five that will be of most use and then score yourself 1-5 against these skills. The list is not comprehensive, so add skills that seem relevant to you in the spaces provided.

Skills

Tick one circle if this value is a priority for you and number the other in order of priority.

Evaluation
Making judgements about the amount, number or value of something

○ ○

Multitasking
Performing more than one task at a time, juggling activities and priorities

○ ○

Listening
Focus attentively on what is said and evaluate the importance or truth of the statement

○ ○

Adaptability
Able to adjust and make changes in response to specific situations and demands

○ ○

Innovating
Creating, changing or inventing new ideas and processes, products or services

○ ○

Teamwork
Co-operation to achieve a common work goal or objective

○ ○

Delegating
Assigning tasks to others as appropriate

○ ○

Team Management
Administer and coordinate a group to perform effectively, setting objectives & assess performance

Financial Acumen
Competent in evaluating financial information as a basis for decision-making

Managing change
Implementing strategies to deal with change effectively

Time management
Plan & exercise control over time spent on activities to enhance effectiveness or productivity

Dealing with ambiguity
Coping effectively with change, risk, uncertainty and volatility

Communicating
Sharing or exchanging thoughts, feelings, information & suchlike in writing, speaking, etc.

Customer Service
Taking care of customer needs with professional, high quality performance

" **Passion is the key to developing in any profession** "

Continue the task from the previous page.

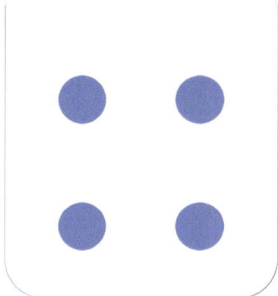

Conceptualising

Formulating and describing ideas and theories, and communicating them effectively

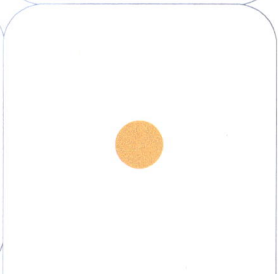

Process Management

Taking a systematic approach to making workflow more effective, efficient & productive

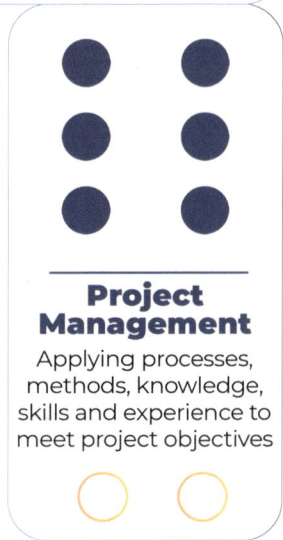

Project Management

Applying processes, methods, knowledge, skills and experience to meet project objectives

Dealing with emotions

In touch with and handling emotional reactions effectively

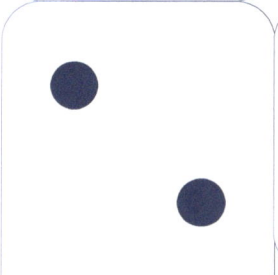

Facilitating

Making things possible, easier or better; enabling or empowering improved performance

Navigating your portfolio life:
Lessons from David Mellor

Imagine embarking on a journey where the destination isn't precisely what you'd envisioned. That's the reality of portfolio careers. You may be surprised to learn that only about 30% of people end up doing what they initially set out to do. David Mellor's journey epitomises this.

"I am not doing what I expected when I set out," he says.

Today, he thrives as a business school lecturer and executive, a path far removed from what he once envisaged.

His advice? Embrace the unpredictable. David likens it to a Darwinian approach: adapt or perish. There will be moments when your plan won't align with market demands, maybe because you were ahead of your time or the market may decide it needs something different to what you chose to sell. Whichever, David emphasises the necessity of staying flexible and open and having the courage to admit when things don't work.

Crafting a solution, not just a service

David's golden rule? Don't look for problems to solve; rather, shape your skills into solutions for existing problems. He advises research to confirm that there is a genuine demand for your offerings. You may not have to change your ideas but simply flex the way things work.

Unpacking your passion puzzle

His experience has solidified a common blend that works: something I know alongside something I always wanted to, as well as giving something back. David prompts us to introspect and discover what genuinely excites us — what 'floats our boat'. The most successful people are those who decide to go part-time doing something for which they are known and that helps them fund research into other interests and pro bono work.

The reality checkpoint

Self-awareness is non-negotiable. David warns that expertise in a subject doesn't automatically qualify one for business. Many people are not good at figures or selling; so understanding the drivers behind your decisions is important and you will need a level of business acumen.

Navigating the transition

Leaving a structured organisation is like stepping into a new world. David highlights the challenge of selling your services as an independent entity, contrasting it sharply with selling tangible property like a house or car.

Mastering the balancing act

With a portfolio career, not all components will progress at the same rate. David emphasises the art of juggling these parts. One can strangle others. You have to cope with that and realise you are successful when different parts of the portfolio are competing for your time.

Strategic time management

Focus on targeted and thoughtful actions rather than spreading yourself thin and exhausting yourself. Be a sniper, not a blunderbuss, choosing the right opportunities in the right sectors to prevent exhaustion and optimise productivity.

Quality networking

According to David, the quality of contacts is more significant than the size of your network. He suggests evaluating your contacts through these three filters:

- For how many do you have 100% mutual trust and respect?
- With how many of them do you have a genuine reciprocal relationship?
- For how many of them are you safe in the knowledge they are always reliable?

This core network becomes a vital source for new business opportunities, as demonstrated by David's experience where 100% of his new business emerged from these trusted relationships.

Regular income assessment

Without becoming overly analytical, establish a system to monitor and evaluate your various income streams. This practice allows you to identify what is working well and what isn't, enabling you to strategically adjust as necessary. It also ensures that you are prepared and flexible, ready to seize new and unexpected opportunities without conflict when they arise.

"The higher your level of self-awareness, the more likely you are to build a career that fulfils you"

Finally, think about acquiring and developing new skills driven by things that interest you and causes that are close to your heart. Business psychologist Michael Greenspan recommends making yourself an "outlier" by building a specific, unique skill set and acquiring the experience that will enable access to niche roles. Greenspan cautions that:

> *"The more specific and unique your skill set and experience, the more valuable your portfolio will be. An expert in banking regulation or solar energy production — or any other niche, challenging area — will find good opportunities to apply their skills. But if you attempt to transition to a portfolio role by marketing yourself simply as a capable, experienced executive, good work will be much harder to come by."*

Of course, this is only true if there is a market demand for your specialist skills.

It's important to establish yourself as being one of the very best in your field of expertise, as that is what enables you to charge a premium price and is what encourages people to seek you out.

Key Takeaways

1. **A portfolio career is about fulfilment:** It's less about earning money and more about doing what energises you, aligns with your values and brings you joy.

2. **Life's too short for work that doesn't inspire:** Focus your time on what truly matters to you and leaves you feeling energised.

3. **If remuneration is a goal, know your market:** To earn from your portfolio career, it's crucial to understand what skills and services the marketplace values.

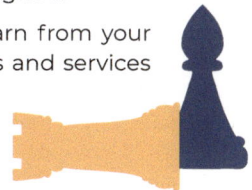

Chapter Five

Creating your portfolio:
Strategic planning

Imagine setting sail on a vast ocean without a compass, chart or destination in sight. It sounds like a daring but also a risky adventure that could lead anywhere — or indeed nowhere at all. This is exactly how a contact of my co-founder at 10Eighty, Liz Sebag-Montefiore, embarked on her portfolio career — without any conscious plan at the outset.

Surprisingly, they're not alone in this. Many of us invest more time plotting our next holiday than thinking about our career path. As a staunch advocate of thinking ahead and planning for the career you want, I urge you to consider this: a well-defined plan isn't a constraining box; it's a roadmap that makes the likelihood of reaching your desired destination far greater.

Too frequently career planning gets shoved into the 'too difficult to do' box. We procrastinate or our fast-paced lives don't allow us the luxury to pause, reflect and strategise for the future. Planning, though it feels instinctively wise, often becomes a neglected practice, despite its clear benefits. We are well aware that failure to anticipate and prepare can unleash a ripple effect of unforeseen consequences, breaking promises we've made to ourselves and loading our lives with avoidable stress.

Why is planning perceived as such a Herculean task? In part it's because predicting the future is inherently challenging. In an ideal world, we'd have a crystal ball — or at least a wealth of information — to guide our decisions. But in reality, we usually have far less information than we'd like. Planning, then, is not just a prediction problem, but also an information problem.

Let's challenge the notion that planning prowess is a trait we're either born with or without. Instead, consider it a skill, akin to creativity or writing, that can be honed through dedication and practice. With persistent practice, we can build neural connections in our brain that make planning second nature rather than an insurmountable challenge.

Our experts say:

> **Sue Mandelbaum:** *Maybe I could have structured things differently, but your life evolves and what I want now is not how I initially set things up. Be open to new ideas and how you think about things and do things in a mindful way.*

Start early by developing your network

It is never too early to start thinking about what you will do when you reach the end of your professional career, whether that is via early retirement, redundancy or a change of direction. In your 30s and 40s, you should be making the connections that will power you through senior roles and give you a solid network on which to base a freelance career.

Note that the network that serves your professional career is not necessarily the one that will be helpful when you take early retirement and start getting your portfolio career under way. Invest time in cultivating a network of contacts who will be able to help you further your career when you move on.

Top tips:

1. Start by making a list of all possible jobs and clients, employers and connections, then concentrate on filling the gaps and developing new connections. A robust network of good contacts is needed to facilitate the start-up of your portfolio work. Look at former colleagues and their connections and at clients, customers, suppliers and all your secondary contacts too.

2. Download your LinkedIn connections into a spreadsheet and segment them according to how well you know the person, how much you have invested in them and whether they have the power or influence to make a call on your behalf that will help you make new connections.

3. Attend professional and industry events to expand your contacts and connections.

4. Keep in touch with people — not just those who may be able to use their influence on your behalf, but also those whom you can help and those whose talents, skills and company you appreciate. This means you will be well informed about what is going on in the marketplace and potential opportunities.

I delve deeper into networking in chapter 8.

Our experts say:

> **Chris Hale:** *I always had a connection with the academic world and had good contacts there, so networking has been important, but people have been unexpectedly helpful. I was surprised at how willing people are to give their time and introductions.*

Explore your options and develop your skills

Once you are clear about what you offer, the sort of roles you are seeking, what will energise and fulfil your expectations and aspirations and provide you with a meaningful and purposeful working life, then it's time to consider your options.

Your next step is to undertake some real-time research into the most appealing ideas and experiment around your existing career. This can include work shadowing to understand the day-to-day activities of a new career, taking an online course or building a blog or website for a business idea you have.

Part of your forward planning should be geared towards finding development opportunities to eradicate the gaps in your skills base. Before you move to a portfolio career, aim to build the skills you will need:

- Treat this like any other role and start by identifying the skills and expertise the very best person would require to be successful and carry out an objective assessment as to how you compare against that putative best candidate. This will allow you to identify any skills gaps you will need to eliminate.

- Make the right noises within the organisation where you work. Seek out personal development reviews and act on them. Spend time with your manager. In effect, seek to negotiate an individual contract whereby your managers know about the skills you want to develop and negotiate with them as to what skills they are prepared to invest in.

- Find projects on which you could work where you could develop the needed skills or by taking relevant secondments or job-shadowing.

- If you are aiming for non-executive director roles it would be wise to ensure you have the experience that will make you attractive to the chairpersons you need to impress. Secure committee experience, possibly via voluntary work for a charitable trust or a role in governance for an educational establishment.

- Corporate social responsibility projects and volunteer projects are also helpful in building skills and contacts and they look good on your CV. Think ahead about where you want to be and develop what we might term the 'aspirational skills' that will get you there. Plan to eradicate the gaps in your experience.

- Make time for reflection after and during each project. Review your performance. What did you do well? What could you do better next time?

- Get good quality feedback from others about what you are doing that genuinely adds value and also where you could improve.

The best way to get a portfolio career off the ground is through a part-time or interim role with your current employer. The smart strategy is to have your portfolio options prepped and well-developed and ready to put into action, so that you can start from a position of strength.

Consider sharing your plans with your employer, suggest a move to part-time or associate work, asking for a retainer for 12-18 months. Promise to deliver your replacement during that time, handing over client relationships. It is my experience that the people who hit the ground running when embarking on a portfolio career have lined up a retainer relationship with their previous employer.

This sort of project offers you the opportunity to try something out for size. There's always the possibility that you won't enjoy the research project, and find that it doesn't give you the benefits you anticipated.

Our experts say:

> **Michele Lahey:** *We don't always know what the options are; we become blinkered and numbers-driven, but it takes all kinds — and talking through options and imagining the possibilities is great fun and all part of founding and grounding your portfolio.*

Get a side hustle

Going down the portfolio career route may be a gradual affair. If you're hesitant about freelancing or starting a business, you could consider moonlighting to experiment with a portfolio career. Volunteering in the evenings and weekends or taking on a part-time job can give you the opportunity to explore the portfolio life and help you upskill, network and gain experience for a new way of working.

You may start out by reducing your hours at your regular job and taking up some freelance work in whatever field you are skilled in or taking on a non-executive role with the agreement of your employer to expand your options.

In the UK, IPSE found that 320,000 workers have a side hustle, that is to say, any activity outside of your regular job that helps you make more money. Technically, this is a part-time job or work done for side hustle apps such as Airbnb, Uber or TaskRabbit.

Side hustles can cover a lot of bases. It might be:

- Whatever you do in your professional career but on a part-time, freelance basis
- A new career option that you are embarking upon on training for
- A part-time role designed to bring in a little extra — waitressing, driving, tutoring
- A hobby or skill that can be turned to profit — making curtains, cakes or car repairs
- A talent for something that you are going to do anyway but might also be a saleable skill — art, music or sport

Talented colleagues have found that they could start exploiting their side hustle while in paid employment (note some contracts of employment may seek to prevent this). It's worth taking a close look at your other interests to decide whether you can add to earnings via something you enjoy and choose to do for pleasure. The monetary contribution may be small but that may not be the point of following this pathway in comparison to the enjoyment derived from the activity.

Whether it is writing a blog, cake decorating, making jewellery, fixing up old cars or property, tutoring maths or piano students or offering research or advice, it might become part of your income stream. If you decide not to pursue the option you will still derive the benefits found in enhancing your skills, making beautiful and useful things, and networking in a different field.

Do your research before you embark on any expense or marketing effort. Things to consider are:

- Your likely earnings rate
- The potential amount of available work
- Long-term sustainability

If your side hustle is what you aim to make your main source of income when you leave the corporate world then you probably need to market test that option before leaving work. Even then, you are likely to find it could take up to a year to optimise a portfolio workload and achieve sufficient earnings, as well as effective sustainability. In addition, as I have pointed out several times, you will still need to stay in step with developing markets and be ready to reinvent yourself as necessary.

The more specialised your product or skill, the more you may be able to charge, but also it is likely that your market may be harder to reach. Will you be able to find enough work at the right price? Be aware that market conditions change all the time, and what seemed like a realistic opportunity will disappoint if, for instance, high unemployment leads to a glut of dog-walkers and curtain makers. For many, working a side hustle in addition to their regular job is a necessity born of the need to meet ever-rising living costs.

For some professionals, working on their side hustle on a project-by-project basis allows them to earn extra cash while building a lucrative portfolio, enhancing their CV and establishing a roster of happy clients. The obvious bonus of having a side hustle is that it affords alternative sources of income, which is always useful. If one area of operation slows down then you have other revenue streams to fall back on.

Side hustles don't always become full-time jobs, but it is likely that side hustlers will prefer this option once the venture becomes profitable enough.

E-commerce company Shopify suggests the following popular routes to building a profitable business in your spare time:

- Create and sell handmade goods
- Offer design services
- Find goods to sell online
- Start an online magazine and sell digital subscriptions
- Teach an online course
- Start a blog
- Start a YouTube channel
- Become an influencer

Some of these can be undertaken from just about anywhere. With a laptop and a wi-fi connection, anyone can be a designer, publisher, teacher or influencer. Side hustles offer you a way to test business ideas and practice in public.

The side hustle can be a way to learn valuable skills and enable growth as a professional and as an entrepreneur. It may offer artistic independence, professional growth and in the long-term a profitable way to turn a passion into a career. However, a word of warning. If your side hustle is a fun thing, your hobby earning you a bit of extra, beware the amount of time you devote to it. Don't let it become a distraction from other income streams or business development opportunities.

Find a mentor

Our options are rarely binary and if one line of work doesn't suit you there are many other opportunities to explore. If you feel confused about the right direction to take then a discussion with a trusted friend, mentor or professional coach can help you understand your motivations to move forward with confidence.

Talk to role models and contact people who are working in the type of career you want in terms of occupational choices and lifestyle.

Mentoring facilitates the opportunity to kick the tyres on your idea. Here are some tips for choosing a mentor:

- Pick your mentor wisely. You need someone who will be both supportive and challenging. There is little point in picking someone who is always going to agrees with you. You need a critical friend. The good news is that people feel flattered to be asked to be a mentor.

- Choose someone who is knowledgeable about the area in which you intend to specialise — preferably who has been there themselves or who could be a potential customer. In that way the mentor assists you in your market research.

- You don't necessarily have to restrict yourself to one mentor. Choose mentors for particular areas in which you want to develop.

- Personal recommendations and LinkedIn are a great source of potential mentors.

Our experts say:

Jeremy Leadsom: A mentor is invaluable when you decide you want to do this. My advice would be to rely on your network and ensure the technical, tactical stuff is in place. Don't pay out unnecessarily for things that probably won't help.

Navigating your portfolio life:
Lessons from Sue Mandelbaum

In the realm of strategic planning, few exemplify its importance better than Sue Mandelbaum. With a multifaceted career that includes consultancy roles, coaching, being a magistrate, school governor and a trustee to two charities, Sue's intricate portfolio might appear overwhelming to the untrained eye. But with a methodical approach to planning, she deftly navigates her numerous responsibilities.

In her last employment stint, Sue had long held a trustee position for a charity and knew she wanted to do more of that. She sought to interweave her professional expertise with her passion for civic participation, aiming to gain as much personally as she would offer. So, let's check out her planning philosophy.

The role of reflection and flexibility in planning

Review, reflection and resilience are the keystones of Sue's approach to strategic planning. Reflect on your whole life, what you like and what interests you, identify the threads you may pick up and develop. Examine in detail your career timeline to work out where to go next and shape something that suits you. Be honest about yourself and what you can contribute. Planning ahead is important, but be flexible and adaptable. Rigidly adhering to a set plan might culminate in disillusionment.

It's also essential to acknowledge that not all endeavours will be fruitful. Thus, resilience, both emotional and professional, becomes crucial. As one transitions from structured professional environments, building a robust support system can make a world of difference. For Sue, this translated to mentors and a "personal board" — a select group offering guidance and support.

Plan early

Sue emphasises the necessity of forethought. If you're eyeing a specific role, especially if it's unfamiliar terrain, you should actively seek experiences that hone the relevant skills. Sue suggests starting small. Engage in leadership tasks or join task forces parallel to your primary profession, slowly but steadily expanding your expertise. For example, if you want a trustee role and have not had any relevant responsibility, then start to work on that, for example getting involved in management or leadership roles or getting involved in task forces.

The networking factor in planning

As her career path evolved, Sue recognised networking as an invaluable tool. Instead of leaving it to chance, she suggests adopting a more structured approach: treat networking as a concerted campaign, diligently recording contacts and interactions. In Sue's journey many meaningful roles have been birthed from unlikely initial conversations. The lesson: Stay open and vigilant. You never know which interaction might lead to the next big opportunity.

Taking the plunge

So, you have done the planning in advance, got everything teed up and an opportunity has presented itself, perhaps in the form of an unwelcome job change or redundancy. You're ready to take the plunge and go portfolio for good. But before you commit fully, do a sense-check by asking yourself these simple questions (and answer honestly):

- Am I organised and self-disciplined?
- Am I confident of my skills?
- Can I focus on a task and motivate myself?
- Can I thrive without a team of colleagues and back-up?
- Can I differentiate my specific skills from those of others in my field?
- Am I sure there's a market for my skills?
- Do I know freelancers/consultants who do this already?
- Do I know who my first client may be?
- Have I worked out the financial impact?

Think about whether it is the right time to make the change. If security and a solid framework are important right now, it is probably not the right time to make the transition. If it is, then it's time to think about the practicalities of setting yourself up, which I explore in the next chapter.

Our experts say:

Mike Grant: *When I left my career in financial services after 30 years, I was fortunate enough to be financially stable, which meant I could take some time to think about what I wanted to do next. With hindsight I probably would not have gone down the training route. What I really enjoyed was the one-to-one client work and real engagement with them and their challenges.*

Key Takeaways

1. **Preparation is key:** As the old adage goes, fail to prepare, prepare to fail.
2. **Start small, move smart:** Don't dive in head first — dip your toe in and begin in the shallow end.
3. **Test, learn and seek advice:** Explore the market, consult trusted experts and remember — you don't have to go it alone.

Chapter Six

Valuing your expertise:
A guide to pricing and practicalities

One area we almost all struggle with at the beginning is how to price our service. It's important to establish your financial break-even point and how much income you need to feel secure and have peace of mind.

So, let me set one golden rule in stone: never undercharge. It's simple but crucial. Let's break it down:

- **Know your worth:** This isn't just about numbers. It's about respect for your craft and expertise. You've invested in developing your skills and knowledge. Now it's time for that investment to pay off

- **Market research is your friend:** Dive into research. What are others in your field charging? This is your starting line, not an arbitrary number you 'feel' is right. Use this data as a foundation and adjust based on your unique value propositions

- **Casual work? Factor in the risks:** If your work doesn't come with the stability of a full-time job, your price should reflect that. No sick pay, no job security — these aren't small things. Your price is your safety net, so make sure it's strong

- **The volunteering balance:** Offering your services for free can be fulfilling and can sometimes open doors. But ensure you're not being taken advantage of by setting clear boundaries and sticking to them

- **Quoting smartly:** Preparing a quote or tender? Be keenly aware of your time. Don't accidentally slip into doing chargeable work for free. Your expertise didn't come overnight; it's valuable and so is your time

- **Safeguard your intellectual property:** Your unique approach, your signature touch, your trade secrets — these are priceless. Make sure they are protected in your contracts and interactions with clients

- **Full-time workload alert:** If you find yourself working a full-time schedule but only seeing part-time pay, it's time to reassess!

Try this useful calculator to determine a daily charge-out rate:

- Work out how much you want to earn in one year/one month
- Divide by the number of days you want work
- Double the rate to take account of the time you'll spend on sales and marketing

Our experts say:

> **Charles Hindson:** *Realise how competitive it is going to be and think carefully about where you will be able to get started. Be realistic about what you are going to find, the types of opportunities that are available and appreciate how the market works. Don't get over-engaged in things that you won't be suitable for.*

Admin angst

It's important to remember that operating a business goes beyond the services you provide to clients. It encompasses various roles: marketer, financial manager, IT expert, document producer and social media manager. Should you handle these tasks yourself or hire help? Weigh your enjoyment of these roles, the opportunity costs and the potential alternatives before making this decision.

Here are some key admin tasks:

- Keep a structured record of your professional contacts. Even a basic spreadsheet serves as a crucial tool to track networking conversations, meetings and subsequent follow-ups. It's essential to nurture relationships that can help catalyse your career shift

- In our digital age, most of us have home offices equipped with advanced technology. It's not a stretch to invest in colour printers and scanners, but think beyond the hardware. Have you evaluated your data storage needs? Are you adequately safeguarding client information as per their expectations in terms of security and confidentiality?

- Ignoring data security can be catastrophic, resulting in substantial financial loss and a tarnished reputation if client information is misused, stolen or lost. Regularly back up important data to a secure, external source that you can access quickly if needed to avoid potential crises.

- Being your own boss can be laborious when you're also the accountant, the tech support and the training coordinator. Those in larger organisations often take these support structures for granted. Striking the right balance between your desire for independence and these additional responsibilities is key to setting a sustainable fee structure.

- Insurance is not to be overlooked. Research the necessity of employer's liability, professional indemnity and critical illness cover in your field. There's lots of advice online and at public reference libraries. If you opt to consult a professional advisor, seek recommendations through your network. Remember, always ask for recommendations!

Your business structure

Once you know your value, you need to think about the best business structure for your needs. The UK Government outlines the most common as:

Sole trader

A sole trader is considered to be 'self-employed'. This means you must register with HM Revenue & Customs (HMRC) for self-assessment as soon as you start trading. A sole trader is responsible for running their business and for meeting the legal requirements that come with it. In a nutshell, you are the owner of the business, entitled to keep all profits but liable for all losses. If you're a sole trader, you need to pay income tax and National Insurance subject to thresholds for profit generated.

Partnership

You and your partner(s) personally share responsibility for your business. Partners share the business profits and each partner pays tax on their share. A partnership agreement document outlines the liabilities, ownership, how profits of the business are split and what happens if one partner wants to leave. Each partner must register as self-employed and submit a separate tax return. In a standard partnership, all partners are fully responsible for all debts owed by the business. You can also have a limited liability partnership. This model protects its members' assets, limiting their liability to however much they have invested in the business and any personal guarantees they may have given when raising loans.

A limited liability company (Ltd)

This is a private company whose owners are legally responsible for its debts only to the extent of the amount of capital they invested. It is a popular model with people pursuing portfolio careers. Setting up a limited company is straightforward. You can do it online and it doesn't cost much or take long. One thing to consider is how you intend to pay yourself. One of the benefits of working via a limited company is that you can take advantage of tax planning measures not available via other business structures. You can pay yourself via PAYE, which has advantages, or via dividends.

The benefits of taking a salary:

- You build up qualifying years towards a state pension
- You can make higher personal pension contributions
- You retain maternity benefits
- It may be easier to apply for things like mortgages and insurance policies for critical illness cover
- You reduce the amount of corporation tax that your company pays (salary is an allowable business expense)
- You can take a salary even if your business makes no profit

"Know your worth."

Most directors of limited companies pay themselves in some combination of salary and dividends, often supplemented by pension contributions from the company.

The main benefit of drawing down dividends from your company is that they are not subject to National Insurance deductions, unlike salaried income. As a director of a limited company you are in control of the finances and can decide whether and when to declare company dividends.

Making pension contributions from your company is tax-efficient; it is different from contributing to your pension yourself, as it counts as an employer pension contribution. But bear in mind the main disadvantage — you can't access that pension until at least age 55. So pension contributions can't be a substitute for salary or dividends, just an addition to them.

Accounts advice

You should discuss your overall remuneration strategy with an accountant. After all, this is the most important aspect of the work part of your portfolio enterprise. You need to consider various factors, such as the current income tax (personal allowance) rates and National Insurance thresholds.

Also think about taxable expenses. You are able to claim tax relief on a number of items and services, providing they are crucial in enabling you to work from home. This might include office furniture, phone call costs, internet access, computer software and rent. However, all come with exceptions and rules determining whether you can claim and to what extent.

It's worth talking to an accountant and getting this right from the outset rather than having to fix problems later.

Take advice about software for your accounts. If you plan to do your own books it's probably best to use something the professionals will find compatible with their systems. It makes it quicker and easier when your accounts are audited. You will need to factor licence fees for software into your budget.

You may decide to outsource the accounting work, and that will depend on how much time you will have available and your ability to pay for someone to do bookkeeping for you. It's smart to understand how the systems work and be able to do the basics, even if you plan to outsource most of the work.

You might want to consider outsourcing other aspects of your business administration. Several of our experts use virtual personal assistants to take care of diary management, travel management, social media accounts and marketing chores. Again it seems smart to familiarise yourself with the systems and protocols in use even if you decide you can afford to pay someone else to take over administrative work.

Navigating your portfolio life:
Lessons from Barry Joinson

For Barry Joinson, a fulfilling life meant more than a pay cheque. It meant purpose and meaning. In his corporate role, Barry felt he was no longer adding value. He yearned to make a tangible, positive impact through his work, but articulating this vision proved challenging.

While he could have easily secured another high-paying job in the City, replicating the life he was eager to leave, Barry wanted more. He desired a career that allowed time for family, personal growth, study and leisure, though he realised he wouldn't necessarily be able to get a City-type salary if he worked for himself. It's this 'me' part that Barry notes as a common pitfall: many individuals leap into new ventures, only to replicate the jobs they left behind, missing the chance to truly centre themselves in projects that are meaningful and that align with their passion.

Embarking on a portfolio career, Barry found this missing alignment. Now, every day is an opportunity to utilise his diverse skills — coaching, consulting and facilitating, writing — in ways that matter to him. He urges others to think beyond being defined by traditional job titles. Now, he says, work is about 'what can I do today that will make a difference?' This perspective makes him feel "like the luckiest person on the planet."

Along the way he has discovered many lessons:

Know yourself

What genuinely works for you and aligns with your reality? Recognise your needs and your attitude towards risk. A variable income can be unnerving. Barry suggests evaluating your financial security. Think ahead about pensions, health insurance and critical illness cover, affording holidays or hobbies that are important to you.

Redefining success

Leaving his City job, Barry aimed to infuse his life with purpose and significance. His vision was clear: make a positive, tangible impact. His mantra: Craft a portfolio career that mirrors your aspirations, values and lifestyle. He encourages us to remember to prioritise our happiness and not simply recreate a version of a past job.

Time and family matters

Barry relishes the time he now has for family, study, reading and meaningful work. It's a stark contrast to his old job where the higher he climbed, the less hands-on and enjoyable his work became. Know that moving to a portfolio career can put pressure on the people around you, so get their buy-in at the start.

Your business, your rules

In a portfolio career, you are your own boss — which means the business's survival rests on your shoulders. Planning is crucial, as is charging appropriately for your work. When you are working you are not developing the business, so you need to charge enough to cover the lulls. Barry highlights the importance of considering how your new direction affects your loved ones. Support, both emotional and psychological, often comes from family as traditional office peer groups disappear.

Navigating a variable income

Budgeting becomes an art. Portfolio working likely means a variable income. You still have to pay for all the things you need and things you perhaps used to take for granted are no longer there, so you have to find time and energy to deal with that. Outsourcing, like Barry did with accounting and administration, can help free up precious time.

Networking wisely

It's not about networking everywhere but networking smartly. Barry started with a scattergun approach but quickly learned the power of being more intentional. He emphasises the significance of building relationships with those who connect with your target audience. He has found valuable business connections at training courses and seminars, amongst like-minded professionals. Reliable business has come via that route. Don't underestimate the time it takes to build your network. People you already know may not give you work once you are an independent. You have to be a credible resource and it can take months for a client to approve a project and then months more to get paid.

Set boundaries and stand firm

Learning to say no is vital. Early on, Barry accepted all offers, but he learned that some work can harm more than help, both emotionally and professionally. The sooner you learn to turn down work that you don't want to do, the better. Most clients will appreciate it if you explain why.

Adapting to client expectations

As an independent, you might imagine you will be able to do things properly and put the world to rights. Barry warns that this is a fantasy; the client wants what the client wants and often what they want isn't 'proper.' That can be hard to come to terms with.

Celebrate your wins

Acknowledge when things are going well and reward yourself. It helps balance those inevitable challenging periods.

Realism and pragmatism

Be honest about your income needs and lifestyle. A portfolio career can offer incredible freedom but this comes with its own set of financial considerations. Relationships are paramount — both professionally and personally. Barry's lesson? It's an enormous opportunity, but tread thoughtfully. Whom you meet on your way up is often whom you'll encounter on your way down.

Accountability and growth

Barry found value in an accountability buddy: someone with a different approach who can offer complementary perspectives. Diversity in your network is essential. "Avoid the guru trap," he says. If you're the brightest in the room, you're in the wrong room.

Visibility and support

Transitioning from a prestigious office to being independent can bruise one's ego when you realise you are suddenly invisible. Barry stresses the need for a strong professional support group. Being visible and active is not just good for business; it's good for your soul.

Barry's journey shows a portfolio career's immense potential. But it also illustrates the degree of self-awareness, planning and adaptability required to make it a rewarding and sustainable endeavour.

Don't forget insurance

You will need to pay for Public Liability insurance, particularly if you have visitors to your premises or carry out work on client sites. It can cover legal expenses or compensation claims if clients, suppliers or members of the public suffer personal injury or property damage because of your business.

Professional Indemnity insurance provides protection against compensation claims if your client loses out financially because of your advice or professional services.

If you employ other people then you need Employers' Liability (EL) insurance as soon as you become an employer. Your policy must cover you for at least £5 million and come from an authorised insurer. You must be able to show your certificate if it is requested.

Take advice from a professional with regards to other insurance. In particular, consider insurance to cover your own health. If you can't run the business you need to protect yourself and the business. Insurance could offer quicker access to medical treatment if you fall ill, safeguarding you against waiting lists. Health insurance is specifically designed to pay for any medical treatment and expenses you may face. The amount is usually paid directly to those it's needed for, meaning you won't receive any funds to help with other costs you may face.

Income protection is designed to replace any earnings, such as your salary, in the event that you're no longer able to work. This allows you to keep up with your usual outgoings.

Critical illness protection can pay out a lump sum should you become critically ill or suffer a heart attack or stroke.

Life insurance will look after dependents you leave behind when you die. You can choose a lump sum or regular payments.

These policy costs, including private health insurance, can also be classed as business expenses for tax purposes. It's worth shopping around, as some health insurance providers offer discounts for self-employed people.

Think about property and other assets, too. Commercial buildings and contents insurance could protect your business premises and contents if they're damaged because of flood, theft or fire.

You may also be able to add additional cover to your policies, such as business interruption insurance to help you if something prevents you from trading (although this is unlikely to cover claims from existing events, such as coronavirus) and key person life cover, to protect you from the financial impact if someone essential to your business dies or is diagnosed with a specified illness.

You can also choose to cover tools, equipment and stock in case they're damaged or destroyed. You may want to consider specialist cyber insurance to protect you from losses relating to damage to, or loss of information from, IT systems and networks. This can supplement any cover in your existing policies and can help with the management of an incident.

Depending on your line of business, you may need to consider business travel insurance or specialist motor insurance. If you are a landlord you may also benefit from specialist cover.

A word on IR35

Changes to IR35 regulations were due to take effect in April 2020, but as the start date was delayed a year as a result of the coronavirus pandemic, changes will be effective from April 2021; changes to the off-payroll working rules came into effect from 6 April 2021.

IR35 will affect you as a contractor if you work for your own limited company. If you work through an umbrella company (a limited company which employs contractors and acts as a third party supplier acting between the contractor and client) you don't need to worry about IR35 as you're already paid through the PAYE system and work under a contract of employment with the umbrella company. IR35 doesn't apply to sole traders but rules for determining employment status do.

IR35 is a ruling brought in to stop the practice of evading tax and National Insurance responsibilities by classifying someone who would normally be a staff member as a self-employed freelancer/contractor.

IR35 is something all freelancers and contractors need to be aware of. Liability for cases 'caught' under IR35 is different with different business structures: in the case of a sole-trader, the liability lies with the client, which is why many are less than keen to work with sole traders.

Think like a business — regardless of what business structure you use for your portfolio career, you are not an employee of the companies you work for. This means that your clients are not obliged to keep offering you work, and you are not obliged to keep working for them. It means that you've undertaken to get the work done, not necessarily to do it all yourself. It means that the client doesn't get to tell you how to carry out your work, provide you with equipment or ask you to do other tasks. If any of these are not the case then there is a risk that the HMRC might view you as 'deemed employed' under IR35.

If you work as a contractor through a limited company you can pay corporation tax at 20 per cent on profits, claim business costs against your tax bill and avoid making National Insurance Contributions (NIC) by paying yourself through dividends. Working as a contractor is often more tax efficient than working via an umbrella company or as an employee of a company. Many contractors who are, in reality,

" Think like a business "

operating in the same way as employees, are intentionally or unintentionally gaining a tax advantage over others working in the same way as them. The government has said that it wants to use IR35 to remove this unfair advantage, and at the same time increase its overall tax revenue.

In the public sector, it is the client's responsibility to determine IR35 status of contractors, and in the private sector, the responsibility sits with the contractor. This changed in 2021 and the liability for assessing IR35 status for tax purposes is no longer solely on the contractor's intermediary but the end business organisation.

When the IR35 changes occurred in April 2021, the responsibility for setting IR35 status and paying relevant tax passed from contractors to the private sector businesses engaging them, as in the public sector. This also means that the 'engaging' businesses will be held liable should HMRC decide status has been incorrectly assessed.

The IR35 changes in the private sector exclude 'small' businesses, however, meaning that contractors working for them will continue setting their own IR35 status.

HMRC can investigate your arrangements at any time, which has the potential to be time-consuming, costly and stressful. They can also go back up to six years and evaluate past contracts to see if the legislation should have been applied.

If you need to have more than one client and one source of income, IR35 should not be a problem for the portfolio careerist, since most are not planning to work full-time or exclusively for one client.

The acid test of liability under IR35 is the ability to prove you have more than one client — non-exclusivity is key. The reality of the engagement holds more weight than the written terms so it is important to ensure your contract is a true reflection of the engagement. There are a lot of factors that are assessed to determine whether you are operating outside IR35 (a truly self-employed contractor) or inside IR35 (working as a disguised employee) and it can vary from contract to contract.

Key Takeaways

1. **Know your value:** Be confident in what you bring to the table — and don't be afraid to say no.

2. **Seek expert guidance:** Professional advice can be invaluable when setting up your business.

3. **Focus on what you do best:** Delegate or outsource the rest — don't try to do it all yourself.

Chapter Seven

Presenting your best self:
Mastering personal branding and promotion

As we have seen, the shift to a portfolio career can bring unparalleled freedom, allowing us to shape our careers around our skills, passions and lifestyle. But with this freedom comes a new kind of challenge.

In a world where you are your own brand, how do you effectively market yourself? How do you concisely and convincingly convey your unique blend of skills and passions, not just as a list on a CV but as a compelling narrative that others will believe in and buy into?

This is where the art of personal branding comes in. Your personal brand is the story that you tell about yourself. It's the image that people conjure up when they hear your name. It's your professional identity that sets you apart in the marketplace — a critical tool for standing out in a crowded field and securing the kind of work that excites and fulfils you.

Once you are self-employed, business doesn't come to you. You have to find it and know where your potential customers are looking so that you can also be there, marketing yourself effectively. When projecting your brand to customers, you will need to communicate the value you offer and the potential you bring to the table. When selling to customers, you will need to communicate how your services have helped others with similar needs. It's vital that you are able to define and articulate your professional brand and then communicate it to the world so that you are effectively exploiting both your assets and your opportunities.

In a nutshell, the clearer and more confidently you can communicate your value, the more successful you will be. In this chapter, we will explore top tips for creating and marketing your personal brand.

THiNK OF THiS AS AN OPPORTUNiTY TO WORK ON YOUR PiLOTiNG SKiLLS

Skills needed to sell yourself and market your offer

Remember the visual in chapter 4. At the top of the triangle was essence and personal brand. Why are you unique and how do you communicate that? I like to think about it this way; what do people say about you when you are not in the room?

Start by thinking about the following questions:

- What reputation do you want to have among your customers, colleagues and competitors?

- What skills and activities will earn that reputation for you?

- What in your portfolio proposition are you proud of and how might you promote that most effectively?

- What is currently available in your field and where does your offering fit in?

By having a good understanding of your talents, skills and experiences it will be easier to effectively market yourself as a professional and stand out in an increasingly competitive marketplace. The top five elements you need are:

1. A good level of self-knowledge, self-awareness and self-confidence

2. Good networking skills and a good-sized, established network of contacts with whom you maintain communication

3. A well-crafted elevator pitch so that messaging to potential clients is clear, competent and convincing

4. A relevant online and social media presence that supports your activities and offering

5. Passion — a personal brand that appeals to your target market and a reputation as a trusted professional in your field. Positive word-of-mouth recommendation means more opportunities will come your way: this is how you get more work.

Networking is particularly important and the problem is that most people don't understand this crucial skill. You need the network in order to source opportunities. Networking is about being the Good Samaritan: it's about adding value and helping people in your network with no expectation of anything in return. Think of it like a bank account which you add to by helping other people so that when you need help it's a good idea to be in credit before you need to start drawing down the favours. Setting up a portfolio career requires you to have plenty of credits at the bank! I look at networking in more detail in the next chapter.

So let's explore some of these further.

Crafting your elevator pitch: you in 30 seconds

In an interconnected world, where attention spans are short, first impressions are more important than ever. Just as if you were looking for a job you need to be able to articulate your offering. This is where your elevator pitch comes in — a concise, carefully planned and well-practised description about yourself that your listener can understand in the time it takes to ride an elevator. Essentially, it's your verbal business card. But it's not just about selling; it's about articulating your value and igniting a conversation that could open doors.

When crafting your pitch, be clear on what you want to achieve. Are you seeking immediate business or simply networking? Your objective will guide your pitch's content and tone. Define your unique selling proposition (USP). What sets you apart from others in your field? What is it about your skills, experience or approach that is unique and valuable?

A compelling elevator pitch should answer three questions: Who are you? What do you do? What are you looking for? Begin with a hook– a statement that grabs attention, followed by your skills/experience and end with what you're seeking or how you can solve a problem. For example: "I'm a digital marketing specialist with 20 years' experience helping corporates triple their organic web traffic. I'm looking to bring this expertise to smaller businesses to help them grow."

Your pitch should sound like you and it should reflect your genuine passion for what you do. Authenticity makes you memorable and trustworthy. Rehearse your pitch until you can deliver it smoothly without sounding rehearsed. Know it well enough that you can adapt it to different situations and audiences. After your pitch, the listener should know what you want them to do next. Be clear and direct.

At 10Eighty we suggest taking your elevator pitch to two people in your network whom you trust and asking them the following questions:

- What have you just heard? (to establish whether you landed the intended message)
- Can I achieve this? (to establish whether they have faith in your ability to deliver)
- How did I come across? (to establish whether you were too earnest or too laid back, over-confident or lacking in conviction and so on)

In a world where time is of the essence, a well-crafted elevator pitch is your key to seizing opportunities fast. Remember, the goal is not just to talk about yourself, but to initiate a deeper conversation and create a connection.

Telling your story

In the world of personal branding, your story is more than a mere recounting of your CV. It's a crafted narrative that reveals who you are, what you stand for and why you do what you do in a way that engages and resonates with others. Beyond your elevator pitch, your story is the emotional connection that sets you apart in a crowded marketplace.

When crafting your story, start with the most fundamental element — your purpose. Why did you choose your path? What drives you every day? Simon Sinek's 'Start With Why' concept is a great tool for this.

Outline the pivotal moments in your life and career. These can be challenges you've overcome, risks you've taken or successes you've achieved. Your story needs to be truthful and align with your actions and decisions. Authenticity creates trust and makes your story relatable and memorable. It's often good to show vulnerability. Sharing failures or challenges humanises you. It shows that you are resilient and that you learn and grow, which is incredibly engaging to your audience.

Structure your story like a classic tale, with a beginning (your background and challenges), a middle (how you overcame these challenges and grew) and an end (where you are now and where you're going).A good story makes people feel something. Use vivid, emotive language. Make people laugh, empathise or get inspired. While your core story remains the same, adjust the details based on whom you're talking to and that what you know resonates with them.

Like your elevator pitch, your story needs to be well-practised but not robotic. It should flow naturally and conversationally. And always end with what you want people to take away from your story. Make this clear and memorable.

Drafting your online presence

Research shows that social media produces almost double the marketing leads of trade shows, telemarketing, direct mail and pay-per-click campaigns. But trying to keep up with all the potential digital channels you can use is overwhelming. You can spend all day on social media if you are not careful. So choose your channels wisely. You can't be everywhere at once and you should try to target your potential clients.

I think a common mistake for those establishing a portfolio career is to rush into creating a website. You don't necessarily need a website. It depends on your product lines and your customers. For many consultants it won't be relevant, but if you plan to make and sell tangible products it could be crucial.

But it is much more likely that your business will come via networking connections.

For instance, we think LinkedIn is a great channel for companies to network with potential employees and other industry influencers. Your LinkedIn profile is much more important than a website as that is where people will check you out. Whenever you follow up an introduction or make a new contact your LinkedIn profile is likely to be checked, so ensuring your profile is complete and that you make relevant posts speaks to your level of connectivity and tech-savvy. It is a useful channel on which to position yourself as a credible expert by posting on relevant groups and discussions. LinkedIn is my go-to social media channel and I discuss this more in the next chapter.

Our experts say:

> David Mellor: *Coming out of a big organisation you may be, to a certain extent, a bit institutionalised, and becoming a business owner is a challenge. The sales element can be a significant challenge as selling a service is a very different matter from selling your house or car.*

As you embark on your portfolio career, take stock of your reputation among peers, clients and competitors. Define your personal brand early and align your actions with this brand consistently. A clearly defined brand, an engaging elevator pitch and a strategic approach to marketing yourself will help you get your portfolio career off to a great start.

Marketing yourself is an important skill. You need to be able to sell yourself, not just your skills and experience. So, to recap, here is your personal branding checklist:

Personal Branding Checklist

Establish your unique selling proposition (USP)

- ◯ Identify what sets you apart from competitors
- ◯ Clearly define your skills and how they apply across different sectors
- ◯ Consider acquiring new skills that align with your interests and complement your USP

Build credibility

- ◯ Construct a CV that emphasises your most marketable and unique skills
- ◯ Showcase a history of continuous learning, whether through formal education or professional development
- ◯ Engage in activities that underline your credibility, such as public speaking, publishing articles or teaching

Craft your elevator pitch

- ◯ Write a concise, engaging summary of who you are, what you offer and what sets you apart
- ◯ Rehearse it until it feels natural
- ◯ Test your pitch: ask trusted colleagues for feedback on clarity, believability and how you come across

Tell your story

- ◯ Develop a compelling narrative about your career journey
- ◯ Highlight experiences that define and validate your skills
- ◯ Rehearse your story, making it fluent and convincing

Draft your online presence

- ◯ Know where your potential customers are looking and be visible there
- ◯ Network proactively, nurturing relationships with people in your field
- ◯ Use social media platforms, like LinkedIn, to enhance your professional presence

Leverage your network

- ◯ Regularly communicate with your network about your goals
- ◯ Practice the 'Good Samaritan Principle': help others in your network without expecting immediate returns
- ◯ Ask: "What does your network say about you when you're not in the room?"

Utilise social media for professional growth

- ◯ Choose platforms that align with where your potential clients spend their time
- ◯ Regularly share content that is insightful and relevant to your field
- ◯ Keep your LinkedIn profile up-to-date and active; it's often the first place new contacts will look

Avoid common mistakes

- ◯ Don't rush into building a website unless it genuinely adds value to your brand
- ◯ Don't neglect the potential of networking, both online and offline
- ◯ Don't allow your social media profiles to become outdated or irrelevant

Navigating your portfolio life:
Lessons from Mike Grant

On the face of it, Mike Grant had everything going for him. He was successful in a 30-year career in financial services. However, increasingly he found himself at odds with his work, recognising that the environment wasn't contributing positively to his wellbeing. He realised he was good at a job he no longer enjoyed.

Intrigued by psychotherapy, Mike embarked on a transformative journey, enrolling in a Masters in Executive Coaching at Ashridge Business School– a programme that aligned with the psychotherapeutic approach he wanted to take. With the Master's under his belt he then started his executive coaching practice.

The initial days of his new venture were far from smooth. He experimented, occasionally finding himself in roles and places, like training and working in the Middle East, that felt misaligned with his aspirations.

But he quickly found executive coaching to be successful, in part due to his strong network and good reputation. He reached out to his network and received introductions and referrals that brought him interesting work. He also ensured that he built relationships with consultancies and other coaches.

Mike believes that if you put in enough work on leads, results will come. Good relationships need nurturing. The big surprise is that it is sometimes easier than you would think, he says. The idea of asking for work can be difficult for some, but he never really saw it that way. Sales is about communications and building rapport, he believes.

After decades in corporate life, Mike appreciates the freedom a portfolio career brings. Here is what he has learnt on his journey:

Self-assessment

Reflect deeply on your true motivations and values. Be honest about the aspects of your job that you do and don't enjoy. The grass is not always greener! In his case, he found himself excelling in a role that he had grown to despise, sparking his decision to change.

Identify your unique selling proposition (USP)

Define what sets you apart from others in your field. How are you different and why would someone want to engage you as their coach? Clarify this unique attribute and show how it aligns with your career aspirations.

Network authentically

Build and nurture genuine relationships, not just transactional connections. Regularly reach out to your network with meaningful interactions. Mike's strong network and reputation were crucial in the early success of his coaching practice.

Experiment and learn

Be open to trying different roles or projects but also know when to step back if they don't align with your aspirations. Learn from every experience, even the ones that feel like setbacks. Mike explored training and overseas work before realising his passion for one-on-one engagement.

Time management

Cherish and utilise the gaps in your schedule for personal reflection, relaxation or strategic planning. Mike enjoys the change of pace his new career affords and values having time to think.

Financial planning

Prepare for a potentially different income level when you leave a corporate role and plan your finances accordingly. Mike was aware he might not match his corporate salary initially but valued other aspects of his new path.

Leverage education

Seek additional training or education that complements and enhances your new direction. Mike's Masters in Executive Coaching was a strategic move that aligned with his interest in psychotherapy.

Protect your wellbeing

Choose a career path that contributes positively to your mental and physical health. Leaving an unhealthy corporate environment was a key motivator for Mike.

While initially worried that he would not get work, Mike's practice is now strong and he is more relaxed. He concludes:

"It creates freedom for me. There is nothing I miss about the corporate world. I find being in institutions quite disruptive."

Key Takeaways from this chapter

1. **Define your brand:** What do you want people to say about you when you're not in the room?

2. **Craft your story:** Develop your elevator pitch, tell it with confidence and share it with your network.

3. **Leverage social media:** Use it strategically to amplify your message and showcase your brand.

IT'S NOT WHAT I CALL NETWORKING SKiLLS

Chapter Eight

Cultivating connections:

The art of networking and relationship building

Picture this: a room full of industry experts gathered for a conference, exchanging business cards and small talk. Now imagine a different scene: a professional, offering valuable insights to a colleague, expecting nothing in return. Which scenario represents networking? Surprisingly, it's the latter — and this is where our exploration begins in this pivotal chapter.

When the topic of indispensable portfolio career skills arises, one contender consistently stands out among our experts: networking. In fact, this chapter might just be the most vital section of this book, and I urge you to lean in and listen closely. For the problem is that most people don't understand networking.

Forget the cliché of conference hopping and schmoozing with the great and the good. Instead, understand networking as a paradox: it is fundamentally all about helping others. It's adding value with no thought of reciprocity.

As you venture into establishing a portfolio career, networking takes on an even more critical role. A study of portfolio careerists (conducted by exec-appointments. com) found that the two most important elements to their success were networking (57%) and self-marketing (20%). Think of this in terms of Pareto's law: 80% helping others and 20% self-marketing.

There are a number of ways to add value for connections:

- Be known as a go-to person for making introductions
- Have a clearly defined brand. "I am someone who knows a lot about ....."
- Be approachable
- Promote how you help people but be careful you are not seen as a self-promoter

Your network should be more than a list of contacts: it should be closely aligned with the services you aim to offer. You should be known in the right circles, by the right people, so that you can sell in to the market you want to target.

But simply being known isn't sufficient. Recall my previous discussion about 'banking credits.' Every act of genuine assistance you offer adds to your 'account,' gently nudging the scales of reciprocity. Those you've aided are more inclined to return the favour when the time is right.

Constructing such a network is no overnight feat; it's a marathon, not a sprint. Patience and persistence are your allies here, so be sure to factor this into your timeline as you lay the foundation for your future.

The 6 Rs of good networking:

1. Relationships are at the core, so make time to build and maintain them
2. Reciprocity is key, so think in terms of 'what can I offer?' Rather than 'what do I want?'
3. Record your calls, meeting and interactions with your contacts in a suitable database for future reference
4. Recommendations: make them to people and for people whenever you can — what goes around comes around. Help others and they will be more likely to help you at some future point
5. Relay information whenever you come across something that may help or interest one of your contacts
6. Reconnect at appropriate intervals; you need to have at least three touch points in any 6-9 month period

Networking is not just a part of your work; in many ways, it is your work. Whether your portfolio career is on next year's horizon, slated for your early retirement phase or planned for even later, the time to nurture your network is now. So, let's look at how you can build your network.

Our experts say:

David Mellor: *In terms of networking, quality is more important than quantity. I started from scratch by building a new network and going to events and forums. At most, I found more vultures than carcasses. People who wanted to sell to me rather than hearing what I wanted to offer. I learned from it but decided to invest time and energy in a select group of connections.*

"

Networking is not just a part of your work; in many ways, it is your work.

"

Navigating your portfolio life:
Lessons from Carol Ashton

Imagine taking the plunge and starting your portfolio life only to come straight up against a global pandemic. This was the lot of Carol Ashton, who made the jump just as the COVID-19 pandemic was on the horizon with its various lockdowns. A scary moment for someone who had given up a predictable monthly salary.

Carol's journey into the realm of portfolio working was sparked by necessity but fuelled by desire. A senior HR professional working in a large global law firm, she describes it as exhausting and draining, tough and sometimes lonely. She was on a treadmill and always running, with little or no time to stop and think about her future and her own career plan. While recognising it was about time for change, this would mean a new role and she was too busy to look up and look around for opportunities.

It took personal hardships and a sudden redundancy to push her toward re-evaluating her professional path. With her husband seriously ill, she needed to be there more for him going forward. She was working long hours with a long commute and overseas travel so her personal situation caused a rethink around continuing her career in a different but more fulfilling and more flexible way.

Then she was brought up short by a redundancy conversation. As an HR leader, she had, of course, seen the decision coming but was surprised by the timing. Dusting off her CV, Carol started talking to headhunters, but with the benefit of an 'enforced sabbatical' realised she was at a stage in her life and career where a new role would mean another much the same as the role she was leaving, with the same issues, politics and relentless pressure, and frankly that was no longer attractive. Also, some of the interviews she attended left her feeling low in energy, and this caused her to stop and reflect on why that was.

Eventually she had to get off the fence and is now working independently from her home office, about an hour's commute out of London. Her service offering is executive coaching and HR consulting, either in support roles or on a retained basis for small organisations, as well as for those that need back-up on specific projects and SMEs who do not have full-fledged HR function but have issues where they need the input of an HR professional.

Interim work was not intended to be part of her portfolio, but in the early days she did take on a contract, as the opportunity was good, in a company she respected, and she was able to negotiate part-time hours which allowed the advantage of providing cash flow while building out the broader portfolio of work.

As the world began to open up after the lockdowns, Carol eagerly anticipated in-person collaborations once more and is now enjoying the variety a portfolio career brings. Here is her advice for embracing a portfolio career.

Network actively

In exploring her options, Carol says she had coffee with anybody who would meet up with her. She notes that people were extremely generous with their time and their advice. She got lots of tips and notably nobody she spoke to regretted making the transition to a portfolio career, albeit they also gave health warnings about losing corporate support, the risk of loneliness, peaks and troughs in workload and financial security, and the chaos that diary management can become! A surprise was that a lot of fruitful relationships are new ones, which has enabled her to spread her wings into other industries other than professional services where she spent most of her corporate career. No referral or personal introduction has ever resulted in a wasted conversation. Much of her new work comes from second level network connections.

Be selective

Turning work down is a dilemma, but if you either don't have capacity or the role does not hit your sweet spot, then recognise you would probably not deliver your best work. You are going to have to say 'no' to someone at some time. Your reputation with the client is better preserved by introducing them to someone who will do a great job for them, leaving you free to take up projects that are more aligned to your experience and interests. This, of course, can work in the other direction too, and Carol has been happy to take on work that was referred to her by contacts who were not available/not right for a particular job.

Dive in but plan to evaluate

Immerse yourself in the new career path but set a timeline to review and reflect. Ask yourself, is this working well or do you need a Plan B? Treat your portfolio career like any other project and be realistic.

Balance work and life

Establish boundaries to prevent overwhelming yourself, especially when working from home. Remember that you now have control over your time, so use it wisely. Delegate where necessary. Carol does her administration because she's a self-confessed control freak but she has an accountant and IT help. Recognise your strengths and outsource accordingly.

Adapt and learn

Be open to opportunities and let your experiences shape your path rather than getting caught up in meticulous planning. Use the flexibility of portfolio work to engage in professional development, keeping your skills sharp and staying ahead of industry trends.

Carol's journey shows that sometimes, life's unexpected twists pave the way for the most fulfilling adventures. For those standing on the precipice of change, she shows that with resilience, adaptability and a strong network the world of portfolio careers holds boundless potential.

Targeting your networking efforts

The success of your portfolio career greatly depends on your networking skills and the size of your active network. You need a substantial number of live contacts to effectively communicate your intentions and desired roles, ensuring a steady flow of portfolio contracts and projects. My rule of 3: At any one time one person won't help you, one would like but won't be able to help you and one will help you.

I believe for a successful portfolio career you need a minimum of 60 people in your network. So, to repeat, a third won't help, one third would like but can't and one third will. 20 people will be those who recommend and introduce business for you.

Action point: Download your LinkedIn connections *(see instructions at the end of this chapter)* and segment them according to how well you know each person. Have you invested in them, and do they have power of influence? If they make a call on your behalf, will the recipient take it?' Aim for a minimum of 60 people who meet these criteria to successfully launch your portfolio career. Begin your networking early, before you transition into a portfolio career.

This spreadsheet becomes your client relationship management tool (CRM). Collect personal notes about your connections, for example, wedding anniversaries or holiday destinations, as well as professional information such as what you discussed the last time you spoke

Draw up a list of target clients — those likely to buy your services — identify the point of purchase and seek out connections who may be able to introduce you or recommend you to that person.

Winning clients through networking

Securing clients is a key aspect of a portfolio career. It's vital to cultivate your professional networks in ways that are compatible with your industry or sector. Building a solid network is essential for earning trust in multiple work areas, especially when taking on a diverse portfolio of projects.

Action point: Ask your contacts for introductions to others in your field, making your availability known. Now is not the time to be shy! Join relevant forums and professional directories, and research reasonable rates for your services as you work to build your credibility and reputation.

The power of indirect connections

While you may not have direct contacts in your desired field, your extended network could be your gateway to that world. When you are building your portfolio you need your network even more than if you were simply seeking a new job. Weaker ties, people you know less well, often yield interesting results. This is because your strongest ties are with people who share your circle of influence, your contacts, interests and knowledge and so they know what you know. Weaker ties help you reach out into new areas of interest and connect you with a new cohort of connections.

To build outwards, you need to be making contact with people you don't know, with whom you don't already share a lot of common ground; they are the people who can put you in touch with new opportunities. This is uncomfortable for many people but I can only repeat my earlier advice: now is not the time to be shy. Reach out to people, but do so while looking to see what you can do for them. My rule of thumb is only to network with people you like. For many people it is the fact they have lost contact with person with whom they want to connect again. It may be several years since they last worked together. Remembering my rule of thumb to only network with people you like, my belief is they will be delighted to re-engage with you even after a long period of absence.

Action point: Leverage second and third-degree connections to gain insights and introductions into your field of interest.

Investing in key relationships

To construct a meaningful portfolio career, diligently nurture your relationships with key individuals in your network. I firmly believe that there is nothing more important in building a portfolio career than investing time and energy in your relationships with these people.

Action point: Make your interactions with these people systematic, regular and genuine, to the point that it becomes second nature to you.

Network management and reciprocity

As we have seen, networking thrives on reciprocity. Don't be a user, only making contact when you want something. Instead, make it a practice to share information and offer help proactively. In a networked world success depends on how we interact with others. Author Adam Grant suggests there are three different networking styles:

- Givers — those who give to others without an expect for a return
- Matchers — those who give to get something in return
- Takers — those who pretend to be givers, but are only motivated by what they gain

Not all of these investments will pay back — that's the risk you take. However, in my business career I have found that by helping others there will be a payback more often than not. I don't know when or by whom, but there will be reciprocal help. And what do you do about people who owe you a favour and don't reciprocate? There is only one answer here: ignore it and move on. You don't know what is going on with your contact and there may be any number of reasons for their lack of response.

Action point: Follow David Mellor's advice: be a sniper, not a blunderbuss. In other words, be a giver, not a taker. In short, nice people can finish first in a networked world. Make calculated decisions regarding whom you invest time in, pick your moment and ensure your contacts remain willing to help you when you really need them.

Building quality over quantity

In networking, a focus on quality interactions can be more beneficial than sheer volume. Building a bigger and bigger network, piling up the followers, chasing the 'likes' is not the only approach you might take. Less is more.

Action point: Instead of tirelessly expanding your network, emphasise deeper connections with trusted colleagues and consider adopting a 'butterfly net' approach over a 'trawler technique'. Make this part of your long term strategy. Don't put off networking. Start early.

Effective communication strategies

Good communication with your network is important. Make sure you cultivate both face-to-face conversations and follow-up phone calls/Zoom and Teams calls at key intervals for your own learning about an organisation's or individual's needs and priorities.

Action point:

- Sign up to appropriate professional websites and alumni networks
- Consider creating a personal blog, social media accounts and public-facing web profile
- Consider search engine optimisation (select keywords carefully, include video to boost your rankings), use graphics and simple podcasts to increase appeal and engagement
- Use LinkedIn to target/follow clients and put your head above the parapet by adding value for your existing connections and building new connections

Continuing networking efforts

A robust network requires constant cultivation and likely years of maturing. It is a significant pillar on which your business is built, sourcing clients and collaborators alike. Bear in mind that a network isn't about how many people you know; it's about how many will send you information, referrals, leads or customers and help you establish and build your reputation.

Action point: Be known as a person who makes introductions, maintains a distinct brand and is approachable. Always look for ways to add value for your connections. Set yourself up as a useful resource and someone who can be recommended for new business, fresh projects or other tasks. Being the person who takes the initiative and sets up the 'next step' meeting will give you an edge and help you stand out as a well-connected networker.

Our experts say:

> **David Bridges:** *Failure to help sometimes may just be circumstantial, so on a personal level, don't let it get to you, because in reality some of your network will not respond. But don't give up on them; a continuity strategy is important. Keep firing arrows and eventually one will get through the window!*

The role of social networks

Do you need LinkedIn to be a good networker? Yes and no. In a business career there's no denying the power a strong online professional network can have over your career success. Done well, it will give you a competitive edge. But while LinkedIn is a powerful tool for business networking, alternative platforms might better suit those in creative fields.

Having said that, LinkedIn has proved a highly successful channel for us at 10Eighty. So, to recap, use the analysis at the end of this chapter to map or segment your network so that you can identify who is most likely to be of help to you with your career planning.

Your network is your strongest asset in building a prosperous portfolio career. Invest in it sincerely, align your contacts with your vision and continuously expand and nurture these relationships. While social media, particularly LinkedIn, is a potent tool, your networking strategy should be broad, with a focus on mutual support and value addition.

Key Takeaways

1. **Your network is your greatest asset:** It's the key to generating business referrals and opportunities.

2. **The value of your network reflects your investment:** The strength of your connections — and the referrals they bring — depends on how much you've contributed to others. What have you done to support and nurture your network?

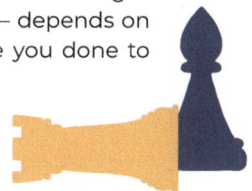

How to...

Download contacts from Linked to an excel spreadsheet

1 Login and in the toolbar on the Home page, click on the 'Me' icon.

| in | Q Search | | Home | My Network | Jobs | Messaging | Notifications 23 | Me ▾ | For Business ▾ |

2 Select 'Settings & Privacy' from the drop-down.

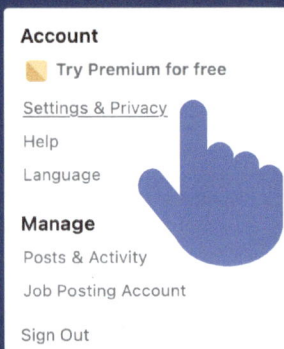

Account
📒 Try Premium for free

Settings & Privacy
Help
Language

Manage

Posts & Activity
Job Posting Account

Sign Out

3 Click 'Data privacy' on the left-hand side.

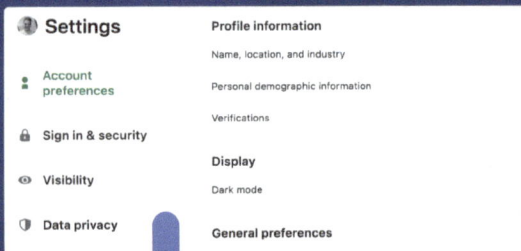

🏢 **Settings**

- 👤 Account preferences
- 🔒 Sign in & security
- 👁 Visibility
- ◑ Data privacy

Profile information

Name, location, and industry

Personal demographic information

Verifications

Display

Dark mode

General preferences

4 At the top, under the 'How LinkedIn uses your data' section, click 'Get a copy of your data'.

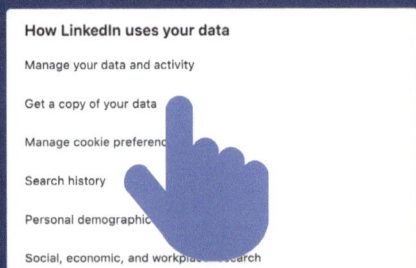

How LinkedIn uses your data

Manage your data and activity

Get a copy of your data

Manage cookie preferenc...

Search history

Personal demographic...

Social, economic, and workplace research

5

Under 'Export your Data', select the second option, 'Want something in particular?' and select 'Connections', then click 'Request Archive'.

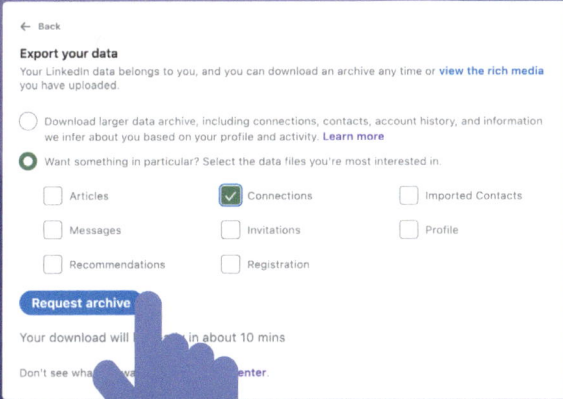

← Back

Export your data

Your LinkedIn data belongs to you, and you can download an archive any time or view the rich media you have uploaded.

○ Download larger data archive, including connections, contacts, account history, and information we infer about you based on your profile and activity. Learn more

● Want something in particular? Select the data files you're most interested in.

- [ ] Articles
- [✓] Connections
- [ ] Imported Contacts
- [ ] Messages
- [ ] Invitations
- [ ] Profile
- [ ] Recommendations
- [ ] Registration

Request archive

Your download will [be ready] in about 10 mins

Don't see what [you] [want?] [visit help] center.

You will need to wait approximately 10 minutes.

You will receive an email from LinkedIn telling you the download is ready (you may need to check your spam folder) titled 'Download your data archive using this link'. Click this link to download your connections in an Excel.

Then in excel...

The document should now be in your downloads folder.

In the document, create three columns:

1. How well do I know this person?

2. Have I invested in them?

and

3. Do they have power of influence? *i.e if they make a call on your behalf, would the recipient take it?*

Then score each person 0-3 in each of these columns, with 0 being low, and 3 being high.

See our example below.

First Name	Surname	Email Address	Company	Job Title	Date Added	How well do I know this person?	Have I invested in them?	Do they have power of influence? i.e if they make a call on your behalf, would the recipient take it?
Anita	B		10Eighty	Business Support Coordinator	11-Jul-23	1	1	1
Daniel	Cook		10Eighty	Project Manager	16-Jun-23	2	2	1
Harold	Mandel		10Eighty	Career Coach	17-May-23	0	0	3
Richard	Class		10Eighty	Mentor	09-Feb-23	0	0	3
Samantha	Joyce		10Eighty	Business Support Coordinator	27-Jul-21	2	2	1
Nigel	Williams		10Eighty	Career Transition Coach	29-Jan-21	1	0	3
Michael	Moran	michael.moran@10e	10Eighty	Chief Executive and Founder	28-Jan-21	3	3	3
Clare	Endicott		10Eighty	Career Coach	05-Jan-21	0	1	3
Peter	Collinson		10Eighty	Career Coach	11-Nov-20	1	1	3
Josephine	Green		10Eighty	Associate Career Coach	03-Nov-20	0	0	3
Liz	Sebag-Montefiore		10Eighty	Co-Founder and Director	26-Jul-20	3	3	3
Shannon	Rowlands		10Eighty	Business Support Manager	20-Jul-20	3	3	2
Hannah	Nash		10Eighty	Business Development Executive	21-Feb-18	3	3	3

WORKING LATE AGAIN

Chapter Nine

Mastering the clock:
Effective workload and time management strategies

Do you ever feel like a juggler with all eyes on you as you try to keep multiple balls in the air? Well, if you thought it was bad in your corporate career, try doing it when you are managing numerous roles. If networking is the most important skill you need to develop then impeccable time management is right on its tail. Letting just one of your juggling balls drop can disrupt your entire rhythm. And it is likely to become harder as you become more successful.

According to happiness researcher and author Ashley Whillans, eight in 10 people do not have the time they want each day. She talks about a time "famine" — a collective failure to manage time. This is so bad, she says, that time stress has a stronger negative effect on happiness than being unemployed.

When you don't have the tools and support around you that you are used to in corporate life, then you need to be all the more aware of this time stress. Don't underestimate the upheaval of the transition from corporate life to self-employed status. Things you took for granted you will now have to do yourself. And they all eat into your time.

Of course, one of the most attractive aspects of changing to a portfolio career is the opportunity to engage in other stuff — the fun stuff and the giving back stuff. We are not simply pre-set to do just one thing. We change over time and our careers should reflect our creative instincts, diverse interests and developing enthusiasms.

Going portfolio is about creating a working style that reflects the way your mind works and the way you want your life to be by following multiple passions, rather than concentrating on just one. If you are the kind of person who is always interested in a range of different things, the portfolio lifestyle is a great way to stay engaged and energised at work, and to share your range of interests with the world.

Broadly, however, we have found that the experience of people who have achieved a portfolio career is that there is far too much to do and they find themselves working longer hours and working harder. You are working for yourself, so finding the right balance can take time. You will need to flex and adapt.

So, you'll need to be self-disciplined with effective time management skills. It's important to be ruthless about organising how you spend your time. Start by talking to people who already have portfolio careers. Ask them:

- What worked for you?
- What would you do differently?
- What advice can you offer?

I did just this with our 10Eighty associates and a number of consistent lessons emerged:

1. Set clear boundaries

Although you are enjoying a boundaryless career, you do need to ensure that you are not overwhelmed with too many projects and that you give yourself time and space to pursue personal interests and self-development. Planning your time and projects is key to success. Set clear boundaries about what days you spend on projects. A well-defined schedule helps maintain focus and ensure each role receives its due attention.

2. Guard your calendar

Don't let your calendar develop a life of its own! External factors can easily hijack your time. Plan your ideal mix of time for client meetings, networking, researching projects, strategic decision making, mentorship sessions and personal reflection. Develop a plan to build these all into your schedule.

3. Follow the 'one plus one' rule

This is one of my mantras, so do remember it. For every day spent delivering work, dedicate an equal day for marketing. So, to illustrate, if you want to be remunerated on 100 days a year, you need to allow an additional 100 days for marketing. This ensures a balanced inflow of opportunities throughout the year.

4. Embrace support systems

You are going to need a diary management system and a 'to do' or work management system, whether electronic, paper or cloud based. Don't be afraid to contract out services which you need to be successful. While it's important to learn new skills, you also need to recognise what doesn't energise you and then find a way to get the support so you can concentrate on what's important to you. For example, if you've been accustomed to a corporate support structure, consider hiring a virtual PA or outsourcing tasks that don't resonate with your core strengths.

5. Seek balance

It's a challenge to ensure that time management and work planning systems work for you rather than dictating your every move. Ensure you allocate time for both work and personal pursuits. If your schedule consistently pushes out personal commitments, it's a sign to re-evaluate, or else you will find yourself back on the treadmill. Be sure to plan for 'me' time, downtime and holiday time. All work and no play won't work long-term. The whole point of going portfolio is to have better control over your time and work. When you are your own boss, there's nobody else to send you home when you've been too long at the office.

When you start on your portfolio career, you may find you have more downtime than you expect. Charles Hindson, who transitioned to a portfolio career, likens it to being an actor. "A lot of resting while building your portfolio." Be honest with yourself. If you think you will write a great novel between consulting projects that's great, but only if you actually make time to write and put some effort into crafting your masterwork will you see the reward of mixing business with leisure. Plan how you will establish a package of activities that will really suit you, the mix and the commitment that fits your lifestyle and meets your aspirations.

One area it is easy to forget about is continuous learning. However, the importance of self-investment can't be over-emphasised. Failure to stay current will inevitably lead to obsolescence. There's nothing sadder than someone telling you how it used to be! Stay updated with industry trends. Regularly revisit blogs, follow experts and attend conferences to keep your skills and knowledge fresh. And don't forget to factor in the time you will be spending travelling for work and attending work-related events.

With so much to juggle it can sometimes feel overwhelming, especially if you work from home and there is a long list of other things you could be doing. With today's many distractions, being disciplined is crucial. Procrastination is the enemy of a portfolio career. We procrastinate because of three key factors: the absence of good habits and systems (poor discipline), intolerance for particular emotions (like anxiety or boredom) and our flawed thinking patterns.

If you tend to procrastinate, I recommend reading the work of psychologist Alice Boyes. Below are some key lessons from her article in Harvard Business Review (May-June 2022) that we share on our Coaching App.

Strategies to tackle procrastination
Schedule your deep work consistently

Deep work is defined as focusing on your most important long-term project. It might entail, say, crafting a business strategy, doing complex data analysis or writing a book. Deep work is generally challenging, but doing it consistently each day, in a regular pattern, will make it less so.

Habits make sequences of behaviour more automatic. You shouldn't attempt to do deep work at 11:00 in the morning one day and 3:00 in the afternoon the next. Even if the exact time you settle into it isn't the same, your deep work should fit into your day in the same pattern.

Create a system for starting new tasks

What about responsibilities you're handling for the first time that feel outside your wheelhouse? You'll be less likely to put novel tasks off if you have a master system for approaching them. The steps you take when you encounter something new will become their own type of habit, which will reduce decision fatigue about how to start.

Disentangle your feelings

Accurately identifying your emotions — something psychological researchers term emotional granularity –will help you manage them. When it comes to procrastination, it's also useful to analyse how much each emotion is affecting your attitude toward a task. For example, you might find that writing a presentation for a potential client provokes anxiety at a level of 8 on a scale of one to 10, resentment at a level of 6 and boredom at a level of 4. Once you've determined that, you can then address the emotions individually. The rating system will help you evaluate how effective you are at minimising them. When a task bores you, schedule a reward for completing it or do it in a more fun way—for example, with teammates you like.

Use self-compassion to overcome strong negative memories

Sometimes the emotions we have about a task are driven by a prior experience. A lot of compelling research shows that you can heal these emotional wounds with compassionate self-talk. Find and then reuse self-talk that works for you.

Reverse brainstorm

When applied to procrastination, it involves considering what you would do to make your task impossibly hard or something you'd really want to avoid doing. Once you have those answers, you then come up with their opposites, which will make you feel less blocked.

The reverse of procrastination is taking on too much, and learning to say no is a vital skill to have when self-employed. It is often hard to say no, especially when you worry about offending the client. So, how can you say no respectfully?

Well, imagine receiving an email from a potential new client that is tempting but slightly outside your niche, or your schedule is already packed with prior commitments. Rather than turning it down with a generic 'I'm too busy' it is best to craft a thoughtful response thanking them for considering you for the interesting project but pointing out that you are deep into some commitments that align more directly with your specialised expertise and you wouldn't want to offer any less than your best. And then recommend someone else if you can. This is much more likely to elicit a positive response from the potential client — and a call back in the future!

The support you have and need

I recall a client who had assumed his wife was going to become his executive assistant, only to discover her main objective was to get him out of the house so that she could continue with her own portfolio of activities. The moral of this story is not to make assumptions about support from your nearest and dearest. That's a recipe for disaster as well as being disrespectful.

It's important to understand the dynamics of working from home and set expectations with family. Finding yourself at home can be a jolt at first. You'll miss the watercooler moments and office politics and you can't use family as a sounding board in the same way you could with colleagues.

Don't underestimate the effect that going portfolio may have on your partner and family. You may be sanguine about the idea of a measure of ambivalence around income flow, but will those around you feel the same? For some of us that is a choice — if we don't have the commitment of a mortgage or school fees we can perhaps afford to take more risks than others.

You will need to manage the transition to this new way of working with those people who are also affected. Communication is a skill you have been cultivating for your whole career. Don't fail when it comes to negotiating with your family. Their opinion should count and you may be relying on them for support and back-up in the future. Be reasonable and realistic about the support you can call on from those closest to you.

Our experts say:

Barry Joinson: *Initially I took everything offered, but then learned that some kinds of work will do nothing but tear out your heart and leave you with a bad reputation. The sooner you learn to turn down work that you don't want to do, the better. Most clients will appreciate it if you explain why.*

" understanding why and when to say no is key to long-term success "

Navigating your portfolio life:
Lessons from Michaela Henshaw

Embracing the power to say 'no' is something Michaela Henshaw learnt early on. A seasoned portfolio professional, Michaela quickly realised that envisioning a plan and its flawless execution were two vastly different things. Agility, resilience and an intuitive ability to adapt became her watchwords. And understanding why and when to say 'no' is key to long-term success, she says.

"If a given project doesn't fit with your long-term plan and desired schedule then let it go. This is a different way of working and you have to think about your time and work in a different way. You are the only person who sees your 'big picture' in terms of what you enjoy doing and what you want your schedule to look like, so you need to take control. Sometimes that means you have to say 'no'. You have to learn to be particularly brave and say no if you don't have the time in your schedule for a piece of work that you find exciting," she advises.

As Michaela has navigated her way through the shifting sands of portfolio work, she has gleaned valuable lessons in addition to mastering your time. Here, she shares her key ones:

Prioritise wellbeing

Resilience is crucial. Organise and structure your work in a way that doesn't compromise your physical, mental or emotional health. Your energy level is the real driver, so taking care of yourself is a priority. Look for ways to boost your energy, both short-term and long-term. Again, you need to learn when to say 'no', particularly if it will be stressful or does not align with your skills and aspirations.

Seek clarity and ask for help

Coping strategies involve clarity about what you are comfortable with and the things you are less familiar with. Don't hesitate to tap into your network for guidance when navigating unfamiliar territories. Whom do you have in your network to help you with the new things you are dealing with or who can give you pointers and advice to navigate new fields and areas?

Strategic planning

Planning is crucial, both in terms of work and free time. When working from home, set distinct boundaries between professional and personal time. Put steps in place to protect your 'me' time. A long-term rolling plan can ensure you don't overcommit and always have time for breaks.

Never neglect networking

Your schedule has to constantly build in networking time so that you don't neglect your future pipeline of business. Dedicate consistent time for this to ensure a steady flow of opportunities.

Map expectations

Before committing to any project, discuss clear expectations, outcomes and timelines with clients. Make sure you have done enough planning to see if it is realistic. Sometimes, you have to be brave about pointing out that if a specific outcome is required then the timescale or the output may need to be adjusted. Such clarity will ensure you don't over-promise and can deliver the best results.

Look after your health and work-life balance

A health scare prompted David Bridges to rethink what he wanted to do and what was important to him on all levels. After working at senior level for some 20 years and contemplating the end of a full-time executive career, he decided he didn't want to retire at 52 but would rather work at a lower intensity for a longer time while seeking improved work life balance. He was a little bored with just doing the one thing and wanted a more peripatetic way of working and the variety involved in a portfolio career.

David decided to pursue twin strands of non-executive director roles and consulting. In time, he secured a non-executive director role and has established useful connections with chairmen in fields that interest him. The consulting side was a success — he had good contacts and always worked hard at networking. His customers ranged from pretty large to tiny, all from existing contacts, which he admits might be a worry for the future, but he has a strong network and maintains relationships with contacts.

In his portfolio career, David achieved a better work-life balance. He said it was not optimal because it was a strong learning curve but in the first year he took more holiday than ever previously. The new lifestyle improved his family life and he was less stressed. On the administrative side, he had plenty of time to organise his business, but says managing the diary was the hardest aspect. His wife was involved with this. He notes that it was

"very interesting to see who stepped up to support and help and the people I did not expect would help but who did so; and, conversely, some, a few, who just did not materialise. It was disappointing when they were people I had helped in the past and there has been no quid pro quo".

In David's case, the move brought the benefits of less stress and more family life. However, it's important to remember there are negatives as well. Working for a large corporation offers benefits such as life assurance and medical insurance, so you will need to factor into your plans a contingency for managing health and wellbeing.

Interestingly, during the course of writing the book, David decided to return to corporate life. This serves to illustrate that some people despite the benefits of the portfolio career the allure of a well-paid, senior corporate jobs with all the associated benefits and status are just too good to turn down. Some people find it difficult to jump off the corporate merry go round.

It's common sense but there are plenty of ways to help yourself:

- Exercise regularly. The change in pace may give you more free time but bear in mind that exercise not only helps you keep in shape but has positive effects on your emotional wellbeing. A healthy lifestyle will improve overall physical health and energy levels

- Review your diary on a regular basis to evaluate how you are spending your time. Ask: Am I spending enough time on me, my family, my wellbeing as well as activities that will build my business and reputation?

- Socialise. This can be a problem, especially for younger people, when they leave the corporate space, so make sure you maintain contact with valued colleagues and peers and ensure you nurture healthy and supportive relationships

The thing about portfolio working is that it starts and ends with you. You formulate the strategy for your winning business and you do the work and in addition you are responsible for support and marketing. You need to establish and maintain a routine but you also need to be resilient and flexible. Alongside your routine, focus on bringing in business and the need to generate income you need to plan ahead to maintain your network and build a pipeline of work.

It can be a lonely existence, so you need to be proactive. You will probably leave behind valued relationships and friendships that you cultivated over many years in your professional career as you exit corporate life. You now need to maintain those relationships as well as building new ones. It is a challenge to stay in touch with former colleagues you saw every day whilst working with them. You need to dedicate time to maintaining these relationships. Furthermore building new networks takes time to build a new circle of peers and colleagues, so persevere.

Our experts say:

Mark Sismey Durrant: *Some working habits die hard. I am working as hard as ever, consistent with how I worked when I was an employee. I thought I would be in full control but if you are naturally curious, which I have always been, then you have conversations with people that open new vistas. Think about health and work life balance and family time. When I stopped full time work I did have to make adjustments and give myself permission to do stuff that was not work. The transition has come about gradually. I probably have had at various times more things in my portfolio than I would have liked but people I like and respect have asked me to work with them.*

Key Takeaways

1. Time management is crucial: While it's tempting to work around the clock, balance is key to a successful portfolio career.

2. Get support for the essentials: Delegate tasks that are necessary but don't spark your interest.

3. Prioritise self-care: Make time for yourself — it's essential for sustaining your energy and focus.

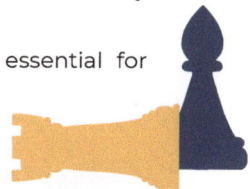

Chapter Ten

Never too early:
Embracing the portfolio career as a young professional

This book is primarily aimed at those who have enjoyed a successful corporate career, have some level of financial independence and who are now seeking to build a portfolio career in their fifties and sixties. That said, in this chapter I want to address the question of whether it is possible to build a portfolio career in your twenties and thirties, at a time when people are at the start of their careers.

The expectations of young people in regards to what they want from work and employment have changed and are still changing. The pandemic only added new layers of complexity to the picture. Younger workers are attracted to new and flexible working environments, such as flatter structures, no fixed desk, access to cafés and sports facilities and spaces that foster creativity. They are often impatient to progress in the workplace and are likely to be frustrated by organisational bureaucracy and culture that may slow the pace of change.

There is a marked desire for autonomy and independence among younger workers, who also express a preference for wanting a meaningful role in life; to make a difference beyond the traditional role in an organisation marketing products and services. These young workers want to make the world a better place. Additionally, younger workers now have greater expectations of employers in terms of environmental sustainability, corporate social responsibility, diversity and being treated fairly.

It's no longer the case that we regard the one company career as a realistic or appropriate route to success. We now build careers around a number of employers and, often, more than one sector. This is evolution in action; new generations of workers are coming into the workforce who may stay in a role for a couple of years and then leave. They don't expect to serve 30-40 years any more — that's finished. Workers now manage their own careers rather than waiting to be promoted, pensions are moveable and technology has made it easier to learn transferable skills. The traditional career ladder is replaced with what is sometimes characterised as the 'corporate lattice,' whereby lateral moves accompanied by longer tenure in a given role and steeper jumps between roles.

This generation of workers has grown up with universally accessible technology and, perhaps more importantly, social media platforms like Facebook, Instagram, LinkedIn and TikTok, which have given them a voice to comment on whatever they feel fit to do, 24/7.

In short, the hierarchical nature of traditional career paths isn't appropriate or comfortable for many of these young workers. This is within our personal experience. Doug Reynolds joined 10Eighty as a freelancer. We were one of his clients. One day, out of the blue, Doug asked me if what he was doing constituted a "proper career?"

My answer was: absolutely. This is your career, tailored to fit your lifestyle, resources and expectations. What could be better?

An international survey by Deloitte found 64% of millennials would consider taking on side gigs alongside full-time employment. It says:

"The growth of industry 4.0 technologies, from robotics and the internet of things to artificial intelligence, has altered the nature of work, while political upheavals challenge the established world order."

The gig economy gives young people a whole range of opportunities to try out all sorts of work and ways of working, particularly as they are unlikely to have the expense of running a home and so on. They can pick and choose when they work so that they can balance studying and exams with saving up some money.

If career paths are no longer hierarchical and unidirectional then a competency-based career is more likely to deliver a wide variety of career moves across multiple departments and work areas. Organisations need to recognise that they need to help each employee flourish as well as to strive to balance the demands of their role and the rest of their lives. The key is to give them the autonomy to do so. While inclusion and collaboration remain important to most of us, we also seek increased flexibility, better work-life balance, and self-authority.

What I am advocating here is a "squiggly career" as outlined by Helen Tupper and Sarah Ellis in their best-seller guide to navigating work in a way that suits you. Put simply, careers are no longer straight line, upward directed, single route, no longer aligned to one employer and no longer dependent on being an employee. Today it is all about the joy of trying new things, working it out and making it up is part of all of our working futures. Squiggly careers ask us to answer some important questions:

- What am I good at?
- What do I stand for?
- What motivates and drives me?
- Where do I want to go in the future?

Young workers may find it difficult to even make a start in the world of work that we took for granted 20 years ago. Pursuing a portfolio career is often an economic necessity as work becomes more like a series of encounters than an enduring relationship. So is it possible to embark on a portfolio career on leaving school or university? The answer is yes, if you have a skill set the marketplace wants to buy. And while that is unlikely at such an early stage of your career, it's not impossible. What you need to do is to give careful thought to building expertise in areas that interest you. Let's examine how to do just this.

Step One: Start early and practise through portfolio

You can't start too early building the skills and network that will give you a foundation for a successful working life. Many a successful entrepreneur started with a side hustle while they were still at school or college — designing computer games, blogging or trading online.

Some people may feel that portfolio working is not a real career but if you are working, building expertise and a network of contacts then you are building a career. You probably need to work, you probably want to work and while it is a hard start in life it will allow you to tailor your career to your opportunities and aspirations.

But the honest truth is that most people are not good at career planning and, in fact, many start their working life with little idea of what they want from their career. For some it may take several unsatisfactory roles for them to work out what they don't want to do! Most people let their careers just happen. They fall into jobs that are offered and stay because they don't focus on what really matters and what will get them where they want to be. It is my assertion that most people spend more time planning their next holiday or choosing an iPad than they spend thinking about their next career move.

If you don't have a vocation or a burning ambition to pursue a particular course then portfolio working is as good a route as any by which to explore your options. If you choose to pursue a talent- based career as an actor or photographer, say, then at the outset you will almost certainly need other work in order to support yourself. A job at the supermarket may be something you take on to make some money while you pursue your dream job, but in reality you may, in time, find that the retail sector is a good career option. There's a lot to learn when you are starting out and it's wise not to cut yourself off from possibilities and opportunities.

Step Two: Take ownership of your career

It may not feel initially like a career, but you should treat your portfolio of roles like a career. Do think about a career plan. The sooner you start building experience and making contact with a network to support your aspirations the better. Your plan isn't set in stone; review regularly and evaluate what you have learned about yourself and what you want from your career.

It is your responsibility to manage your career. Don't be beguiled into thinking that loyalty will pay off; organisations are usually ruthless with regards to disposing of assets they no longer need. They usually can't afford to be philanthropic towards contractors who are not required.

Be proactive — opportunities to advance don't always fall into your lap so seek them out. To succeed, you have to take charge of your career and market yourself as a product and campaign accordingly, whether planning your next move, climbing the career ladder or reinventing your life.

We recommend a regular career MOT. Take time out and conduct a self-appraisal on a regular basis. Is your career on track? Is the direction you are taking still the right one? As a potential asset, are you appreciating or depreciating? Fixing on a new direction is harder but playing to your strengths is a good bet.

Step Three: Become a problem solver

The great conundrum of recruitment is that you only get hired for the skills, knowledge and expertise you already have. So at the outset you face a Catch-22 situation: how do you develop those aspirational skills and how do you close the gaps in your experience?

The right spread of skills and depth of experience are what will carry you through to success in your chosen field. This applies whether you want to achieve a chief executive role with a multi-million pound quoted company or just a more senior role in the supermarket where you work three days a week to supplement your income from writing or painting or teaching yoga.

There are always potential employers willing to take a chance on an outlier, on someone doing something different or taking a new approach to challenges and problems. The key is to aim to be a problem-solver and to articulate this when approaching people about jobs, whether they be full-time or portfolio.

Step Four: Develop portable skills

Problem solving is just one skill that all organisations want. Survival is about ensuring continuing appeal to employers over the long run. Do you have portable skills that will carry you through your short-term career goals and your long-term plan? Working in the gig economy means you need to upskill regularly to stay employable over a longer working life and will probably need to spend your own time and money to do so.

Those most likely to succeed are those who have newly required skills — perhaps skills that have emerged in the last few years and where, at present, demand exceeds supply, for example data scientists, machine learning engineers, algorithm experts and anything related to artificial intelligence.

Take a holistic view of personal development. Don't just learn for the sake of your job but for the sake of your life. Develop curiosity. Learn to question more. In a changing world, the ability to adapt is going to be increasingly important.

"This can be the starting point for a career journey that will enhance your life."

Step Five: Build a network

I suspect the single most powerful blocker to a young person setting up a portfolio career is the lack of a network. I can't emphasise enough that it is your network that feeds you and that gives a foundation for your whole career. Networking is a skill that portfolio workers must develop, as your reputation is built on the recommendation of others. A simple introduction or recommendation can put you ahead of the competition when it really counts, so focus on establishing a network that you can rely on for support. The best advice for people wanting to build a network quickly is: collaborate, collaborate and collaborate.

You will not achieve your career goals without help; your network is your eyes and ears. The more people there are in your network and the more they know about your goals, the more likely they are to help you, and the more likely you are to succeed. Talk to people you admire, to your role models. How did they get where they are today? What was their career path? What advice can they offer? What skills and competencies did they develop along the way? Most people like to help; they'll be flattered that you respect their opinion and happy to talk about their achievements and point you in the right direction. But if you don't ask, you won't get.

Use the technology at your disposal — LinkedIn, in particular, is invaluable. But make sure your network is well structured. You need around 60 people who will endorse and recommend you. You will need to identify useful contacts and potential new contacts to target, and invest in them. To do this, you need to add value for them, to be an asset in their network. Reciprocity is key in networking and you need to pay it forward. Make some notes describing what you actually do; think in terms of results rather than tasks. This is useful not only for working out your objectives but for networking conversations. Check out chapter 8 for more on building your network.

Step Six: Reflect

What if you think you are in the wrong space, the wrong job, the wrong career? Is there anything you can do? Start by going back to fundamentals. What do you like doing? Think about your achievements to date and think big; don't be modest. Life is full of achievements, big and small. Give yourself some space to consider how you got into a situation or a role that is not right for you. What can you do about it? What are you willing to do to get what you want? What might you be prepared to give up in order to achieve what you really want from life? Bear in mind that no matter what your starting point, any career can lose its charm over time. Whole new perspectives open up when you open your eyes to what's beyond the boundaries of the world you take for granted.

Things to watch out for

Going portfolio is not for the faint-hearted and so here are a few words of warning for any person looking to start their career this way.

The bank of Mum and Dad

How will you support yourself when you are starting out is a problem for many young people. Well, don't discount the bank of Mum and Dad. Most successful entrepreneurs start with financial backing from their parents. Family money and background play a critical role when it comes to starting up a business. It's one of the primary sources of funding for start-ups, ahead of other options like bank loans and venture capital.

However, if you are lucky enough to have this route available to you, think carefully about putting things on a solid footing. There are a lot of advantages in using family money and connections but bear in mind they are likely to take a close interest in how their investment is doing. These are people you know and care about, whom you see in the holiday season, and that can be a difficult thing because you may feel terrible losing their money. You may well have to work at more than one job and balance your ambition and need for an income stream. It can be hard but if you put in the hours and effort you should find that youth is no barrier to success.

Psychological impacts

Research suggests that the aspects of the workers' lives most likely to be affected by portfolio work are work intensity, work-life balance and wellbeing. Mission and purpose remain key drivers for employee engagement and, traditionally, this was centred on the employer. If you are self-employed, you need to supply your own mission statement. It may be centred on an issue, for example the environment, a social cause or something that reflects your personal values.

As a self-employed worker you often miss out on constructive feedback, as unlike full-time employees, portfolio workers are unlikely to receive much in the way of confirmation of a job well done (important to any worker's motivation) from those you are working with. To get feedback from your clients you need to be very customer-centred (though this is a characteristic that will be an advantage in any 21st century worker) and active in asking for feedback — good and bad.

Bear in mind that human beings are social animals and for many people, especially those in their 20s, work is also a place where you socialise, make friends and meet prospective partners. So, working on your own can be lonely. This problem of isolation should not be underestimated. That's why, for those who work in the gig economy, the shared/ communal work space is so popular. Co-working space enables contractors and peripatetic workers to build social networks.

Beware of concentrating too much on side hustles

As we saw in chapter 5, a side hustle can be a great way to test the viability of the portfolio option. It's a clever way to test and explore new career ideas and their money-making potential, with the added bonus of potentially earning you some extra cash. And, of course, a portfolio career could lead to the establishment of a business which becomes your employer. As you build expertise and contacts you may find that you can slim down your portfolio and concentrate on your favoured area of activity. With luck and good management, your side hustle could become a thriving business.

However, be careful of concentrating too much on side hustles. They can be a distraction. Try not to think too much in terms of the next gig. You need an income stream that will support you and allow you to build in some personal and business growth opportunities. Your best bet is to use your side hustle as a means to combine a traditional career while putting in place the foundation for your first steps towards a portfolio career. Focus on offering differentiated services in order to maximise earnings, and an evolving portfolio based on where the returns on your time look to be the most promising.

At 10Eighty, we firmly believe that a portfolio career doesn't have to be the preserve of someone over the age of 50. If you value independence and autonomy and if you want to follow a passion, this can be the starting point for a career journey that will enhance your life.

It doesn't matter if you fail — the learning experience will prepare you for a more traditional career. Self-investment of any kind can only be beneficial. Lifelong learning is an indispensable tool for every career.

This working world is the new normal, so look for the opportunity and focus on the chance to diversify and use your skills in different ways. Portfolio is not an easy start in working life but for the determined there is no reason why you shouldn't be successful. It may not be exactly what you would have chosen but it can enable a happy and productive life with a lot more choice than those in full-time employment are likely to enjoy.

Key Takeaways

1. Portfolio careers are for everyone: No longer just for grey-haired men, they're a viable option for anyone post-education.

2. Success takes effort: To thrive, you'll need to manage your career, build in-demand skills, cultivate a strong network and develop resilience.

Chapter Eleven

Boardroom bound:
Venturing into non-executive director roles in your portfolio journey

Many people wishing to set up a portfolio career dream of claiming a remunerated non-executive director role. However, the road to this illustrious position is no longer a mere hand-me-down from the era of 'old boys' clubs' or the prerogative of the time-served senior executive, I am pleased to say. The modern boardroom is evolving and getting a non-executive role is the most difficult role to secure as a portfolio career worker.

As our expert Andrew Tallents, founder of The Tallents Partnership, says: "Too often recently retired leaders are advised that the non-executive route is an option. They then feel flattered and start looking for such a role. That's not a good reason to take such a step."

Andrew, who works with business leaders around the world to improve the leadership capability of their boards and senior management teams, advises such people to dig deeper into their motivation for such a move. "You need to know and understand yourself and work with that rather than respond to flattery. Do you feel it is time to give something back? This is about giving back by making a different sort of contribution from that made as a leader or manager. So, be clear about your reasons and purpose and why that fits for a non-executive director role when you are being interviewed, as you will then come across as more authentic and convincing."

We concur, as taking on such a role is a significant commitment and you have to be sure that both you and the board consider it a worthwhile investment. There are three main motivators:

- The wish to make a contribution
- Personal development and the broadening of your experience
- The chance to offer new ideas from experience acquired as an executive director

UK law does not distinguish between executive and non-executive directors. All board members have the same duties and responsibilities. As you contemplate this step, realise that being a non-executive director isn't just a title. It's a serious undertaking which requires self-awareness and due diligence around companies which offer such an opportunity.

The non-executive director is required to be independent of the management of the company, in order to monitor and evaluate a company's executive directors. She is expected to focus on matters raised in board meetings by providing an independent perspective of the company separate from its day-to-day running.

Guidance for getting your first NED role
Consider how you bring value
A board that is functioning well relies on respect, trust and candour, so you need to show how you add value and bring diversity to the table with your talents, expertise, perspectives and experience that will contribute to the board team. Before diving in, introspection is crucial. Ask yourself: What's my unique edge?

The Institute of Directors advises taking stock of your career to ensure that your experience is clearly described by your CV. Bear in mind that the role of non-executive director places great emphasis on personality and ability, not just career achievements, so you should demonstrate your independence of mind and readiness to take — and stand by — decisions.

Identify companies that are of interest to you
Research the history of non-executive appointments at that company and when there are likely to be natural board rotations. Aim to build strong relationships with recruitment firms who advertise roles that would interest you.

Look for small and fast-growing businesses
Bear in mind that you will need to look for roles in an organisation smaller than those you have been working for. If you work for a FTSE 250 corporation you won't get a non-executive directorship role in such an organisation without experience. Don't make the mistake of focusing on large-listed companies. If you are seeking a first non-executive directorship it is probably smarter to aim your attention at small and medium sized enterprises (SMEs) and growing businesses. Smaller companies have just as much need for independent advice and expertise. They're hungry for people who can get them to the next level.

An SME will generally look for a person to take a 'helicopter' and strategic perspective of the business; someone with the knowledge, skills and expertise to ask the right questions, evaluate appropriate strategies and strategically support the business via a broad network of business contacts, industry and sector knowledge or even access to funding. So, ensure you have a network of contacts who can help you target potential opportunities.

Consider training

It could be worthwhile to look at non-executive director training courses. There are a number available, including Institute of Directors training and programmes run by a number of business schools. Such a course would equip you with the latest thinking and methodologies around corporate governance, enabling you to present yourself effectively at interview as you will be in a strong position to evaluate the various risks facing an organisation and how you, as a director on the board, could mitigate such risks.

Communicate your value

Ensure that your LinkedIn profile spells out your value to director recruiters. If you choose to focus on non-executive director opportunities in a particular sector join the relevant trade association, give speeches and write articles for publication. In short, cultivate a reputation for being a serious thinker about the sector and its future. Ensure you convey the same message to everyone at every opportunity. This creates conviction in your story and affords clarity to those who are assessing your suitability.

Finding your role

For the public sector, the Centre for Public Appointments offers roles in the NHS, regulatory bodies, national museums and galleries and advisory bodies. You can register for relevant posts and sign up to their regular newsletter or receive email notifications when new appointments are published that match your requirements.

Often companies use executive search firms to select non-executive directors. There are numerous specialist agencies and headhunters and platforms that specialise in servicing boardroom personnel requirements. There are also networks and platforms that aim to help directors find roles such as Nurole and NED on Board. That said, it's our belief that a suitable non-executive director appointment is at least as likely to come out of your network.

Work on building relationships with several firms and ensure they know that you are interested in a non-executive directorship. Stay in touch regarding your aspirations and be prepared to share your knowledge and views about others by offering to help on searches where you may not be a candidate by suggesting suitable people that the search firm might contact. Such roles also appear in the press, where the recruitment sections of The Financial Times, The Times, and The Guardian are the most likely to carry advertisements for board positions.

Smartest of all is to line up non-executive directorships before you leave your last permanent role.

Our experts say:

Carol Ashton: *Headhunters have been helpful in terms of advice and introductions, but their process is usually role-specific and quite transactional and so you need to be proactive rather than expecting them to keep in touch.*

"

be true to yourself and do not compromise

"

Research, research, research

When you do gain an interview for a non-executive director position, gain insight into the company and some of the issues that are not obvious from the outside looking in. Do your due diligence on the current board and consider any potential conflicts.

Convince the chairperson

Ensure that you can convince the chairperson about your commitment, your vocation, your relevant skills and how you will manage the transition to becoming a non-executive director. Prepare thought-provoking questions and don't hold back on the tough ones. Demonstrate your questioning and listening skills and try to make it more of a conversation than an interview.

What does a chairperson want? Here are Andrew's top four recommendations:

- Curiosity. You have got to be interested in how the business is being run
- Emotional intelligence. Can you manage relationships with executives?
- The ability to hold others to account. This can come from executive experience but too often many executives do not, in fact, hold their teams to account
- The ability to hold back. Wait until your contribution is required. Quality not quantity is the issue. You need to be able to pay attention, listen, observe and absorb a lot of information until it is time to ask the CEO the one question that makes him stop and think — the question that will make a real difference to the approach taken or the direction of travel

Get feedback

If you are not appointed following the interview, ask the chairperson for immediate feedback and take on the learning for next time.

Be true to your stated intentions

When considering non-executive director opportunities, be true to yourself and do not compromise under any circumstances. It is easy to be flattered by approaches for non-executive director roles that don't meet your specific criteria. Think carefully about the first non-executive director role you take on.

As Andrew says, the better you understand your own reasons for becoming a non-executive director, the easier it will be to identify the right role and convince others that you should join their board. This is about self-leadership and about defining your potential contribution and fit as opposed to applying for roles as they come up. Also, consider what kind of chairperson you want to work with.

Navigating your portfolio life:
Lessons from Mark Sismey-Durrant and Paul Mussenden

Mark Sismey-Durrant is a seasoned portfolio careerist and non-executive director who started early. He was asked to stand for election as president of the alumni association at Loughborough University and as a consequence of that was also appointed as a lay member of the University Council. After his three year term as president, he was asked to chair the university audit committee for six years, continuing throughout as a member of council and ultimately serving as a Pro-Chancellor. He says it was a great learning experience and he loved every minute of it. He is still involved as Chair of the Strategic Advisory Board of the Loughborough Business School.

Mark has served for several years on the board of the BBA and UK Finance and chaired the Audit and Oversight Committee for UK Finance. For a number of years, he chaired both trade associations' specialist/smaller banks advisory boards. He has also been a trustee of a number of charities and served on the Development Board for the creative arts charity Create and is a trustee for the Bedford School Foundation Trust. He is a freeman, liveryman and Council Member for the Worshipful Company of International Bankers and served as Master in 2018/19. He chaired its Charity and Educational Committee for a number of years. Much of this work goes on in the evening. Earlier in his career, he was also appointed Chair of the British Icelandic Chamber of Commerce.

If that weren't enough, since retiring as a CEO, Mark has held a number of NED Board roles as Chair of two dual regulated UK banks and Senior Independent Director of an AIM listed bank, as Chair of a Swedish Finance business and as Chair of an AIM listed specialist lender and a privately owned lender.

In contrast, Paul Mussenden began his portfolio career when he obtained a non-executive role at a healthcare charity while still working in a full-time job. After leaving full-time employment when his employer was acquired by another company, he decided expansion of his portfolio would be an ideal way to exploit his varied skills and provide a different way of working, having been at the one organisation for 19 years in a variety of roles. He was very deliberate about what he wanted, and was explicit with others that he was not looking for a job but was interested in consultancy/NED work, specifically in the healthcare sector. Clarity around his aims meant the courting phase was easier, though it would often take 3-4 months or more to establish whether the fit and timing were right for both parties.

Paul was headhunted to the unpaid charity role which complemented his existing experience of working with diverse boards, helped him position himself as a non-executive director and opened doors to other potential roles. His portfolio originally consisted of deputy chairman and chair of the audit committee at a leading life science charity. He holds two non-executive roles at a Canadian public healthcare fund and at two privately owned healthtech companies. Those roles were attained via networking and third party contacts. He has since transitioned from a non-executive to the CEO role at one of the healthtech companies.

Navigating the complex world of non-executive director roles is an art. While both were seasoned professionals who transitioned into this space, Mark and Paul's journeys were markedly different, but both emphasise the same fundamental truths: success is rooted in strategic networking, adaptability and self-awareness.

Networking

Both concur that networking isn't about the immediate gain. Instead, it's a long-term investment in relationships. Mark reveals that many of his opportunities came not from deliberate seeking but because he had made himself a known and valuable presence in his circles. Paul echoes this sentiment, stressing the enjoyment and value of networking without the immediate pressure of securing a job. This approach not only helped them to broaden their horizons but also opened doors to unexpected opportunities.

Prepare for the unexpected

Transitioning to a non-executive director role or managing a diverse portfolio isn't a linear journey. Both professionals found themselves faced with opportunities they hadn't anticipated. For Mark, unexpected projects became valuable additions to his portfolio, while Paul found himself considering a full-time CEO role amid his non-executive commitments. This underlines the importance of being open-minded and adaptive, ensuring that you're prepared to seize the right opportunities when they arise.

Understanding governance is critical

Another resonating theme is the depth of understanding required in governance roles. Many underestimate the intricacies of guiding an organisation from a non-executive standpoint. Mark says, for example it's important to bear in mind that if you become involved with a regulated business there is a lot of security around information shared with you through portals and email accounts which can be complicated and take a lot of time. Both Mark and Paul emphasise the cruciality of understanding the nuances of each board and company culture. It's not enough to bring expertise; you need to mould that expertise to fit the unique requirements and dynamics of each board. That often means acting as a facilitator, a mentor and a strategic advisor, offering broader perspectives beyond just domain knowledge. Mark says many NED jobs want your networking skills and for you to open doors for them. They want to know that you will be an enabler and facilitator on the board and offer a broader skill set and perspective. The ability to help influence and facilitate an effective board culture and engagement is very valuable, as is problem solving.

Work-life balance

Self-awareness and personal balance are also paramount. Mark speaks candidly about the adjustments he had to make in his life after stepping away from a traditional role, emphasising the importance of personal time. He says he had to make adjustments and give himself work-related activities. He has slowed down his speed reading and now reads more deeply and takes on more detail. Mark also talks about the huge benefit of walking his dogs — it is when he solves problems. But he admits some working habits die hard! Paul also acknowledges that balancing work and personal time can be challenging. Both highlight the importance of understanding oneself, setting boundaries and ensuring that personal wellbeing doesn't take a backseat.

To recap, if you are currently in an executive role and looking for a first non-executive director role be sure to have written in formally the number of days you are able to commit to a non-executive director role. Potential NEDs don't always understand how much work is involved and the legal obligations they will be undertaking. Success as an NED isn't just about domain expertise or having a vast network. It's about strategically nurturing relationships, being adaptable to unexpected opportunities, deeply understanding the intricacies of governance roles and always maintaining a sense of self-awareness and balance.

Some words of warning

A NED's workload can be erratic and sometimes taxing. A role advertised as being for three days a month may see you working intensively in periodic bursts. The advertised time commitment is usually a significant under-estimate due to the need for background reading and thinking time.

In a non-executive director role, you're expected to be 'on call' when you are needed. When something serious happens, from a takeover bid to a scandal or disaster, the non-executive directors will be in demand non-stop. If you manage to secure several board roles then you will need to manage your diary effectively.

As with all other aspects of your portfolio, you need to stay in touch with new developments in the marketplace. Ensuring you stay 'relevant' to the changing environment is immensely important. Taking time to inform yourself of changing business context is essential to optimise contribution.

You need to detach yourself from the executive mindset, as that is not what a non-executive does. Some people think the skills they accrued as an executive are the ones they take to the board. Not so. You will need to demonstrate that you are ready to step up to a new way of working.

Our experts say:

> **Andrew Tallents:** *Particularly early in your non-executive career you may not be confident enough to dig deep and, if that's the case, you may end up with a role that doesn't suit your needs. So, be sure to ask lots of questions to ensure there is a good fit. When you do join the right board, you will probably be entering the most enjoyable part of your career."*

Trustee and other roles

The market for non-executive directors is very competitive. Securing a first directorship can be challenging but the Institute of Directors advise that there are some intermediate steps which may improve your chances:

- Become a school governor — the school governor has exactly the same duties and responsibilities as a non-executive director. Providing the independent viewpoint in managing a school, combined with business experience, makes you a more rounded NED candidate.

- Take an unpaid role — as a non-executive director at a charity or not-for-profit. This will show your ability to commit, as well as providing valuable experience.

- Find a mentor who already holds a board role — ask for insights into the working of a board, advice on your campaign, and access to networks of directors as well as personal referrals.

Another way to ease into the mindset when looking for a non-executive director appointment is to take a trustee role. However, Andrew cautions to only do this if you identify with the organisation and feel passionate about it and able to make a real contribution.

If you are taking a role just for the experience then it will probably not help you gain really useful experience. The same applies to not-for-profit roles and school board roles. Some trustee boards are not models of good governance and don't really fit you for the boardroom table.

There is also a danger that if you get one or two of these types of roles you will be pigeon-holed as someone who specialises in quango/not for profit roles.

The role of a trustee is relatively flexible in comparison to that of a non-executive director. Trustees tend to find themselves and their role far more responsive to the needs of the organisation, whereas the non-executive is more likely to have a role very clearly defined with fixed parameters as an independent member of the board.

NEDs are required to be informed and experienced, offering insight and advice to management but not actively engaged in executive action within the enterprise. The trustee role may well involve a more personal contribution to the work of the organisation.

When seeking a trustee role, be sure to explore what will be expected of you and whether the role is for a fixed period or open-ended. Ideally look for roles in which you feel a personal interest and be prepared to promote the success of the organisation.

Key Takeaways

1. **NED roles are challenging to secure:** Consider alternatives like Trusteeships or Board Advisory roles as stepping stones.
2. **Know if it's the right fit:** If you prefer hands-on execution, an NED role may not suit you — it comes with significant responsibilities.

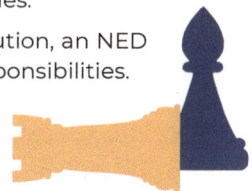

Chapter Twelve

Volunteering, Giving back

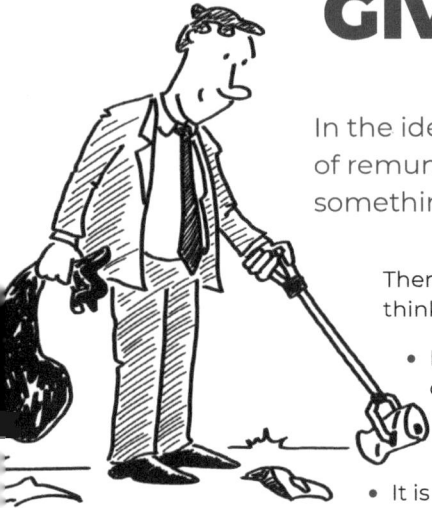

In the ideal scenario a portfolio career consists partly of remunerated work, partly volunteering — giving something back, and lastly time for yourself.

There are three things you should consider when you are thinking about giving back:

- It should be something in which you have an interest or, even better, a passion.
- It should use your existing skill set as you need to be able to add value to the not for profit.
- It is about being a resource for the not for profit where you are volunteering.

The power of volunteering goes beyond giving back. Volunteering is a great way to learn new skills or refine ones you want to develop. It affords access to new networks of people and it builds your competence, confidence, and perspective. While volunteering, you meet people you may not have met otherwise, opening up new worlds to you.

You may be able to develop skills and perform roles you not available to you in your current work or which you need to develop to be promoted to another job or level.

The benefits of volunteering

Many non-profit organisations need willing and capable volunteers; there are always openings. The good news is that you can use volunteering to develop new skills and further your interests. This in turn can help the remunerated part of your portfolio. Volunteering is a really good way of building a network in a different area of interest and expanding your social capital by forming new connections.

Volunteering offers a way to develop yourself, help others, boost your career, improve your mood and reduce stress:

- Develop — learn from being part of the organisation you volunteer with, its mission, purpose and how it operates. You learn from the job you are doing and the staff and other volunteers you work alongside.

- Give back — using the talents and skills you have and by acquiring new skills to contribute. You build expertise and experience along the way.
- Enhance your CV — volunteering offers avenues for career growth that you can boost to your CV and profile, all while strengthening your network and forging new relationships.
- Boost your mood — giving back provides a sense of purpose which contributes to increased self-confidence. In helping others, you feel better about yourself and that boosts endorphins, leading to greater happiness.
- Volunteering means a change of pace from regular work, hopefully doing something you enjoy. Of course, volunteering does have its own stresses, but it's different if it is something you care about.

Where to find opportunities

Start by deciding exactly what you can commit to in terms of time:

- Research: consider your interests and options
- Know what it is you are offering and align that with the organisation's requirements
- Consider how much time to you want to give the not for profit; it should be something you really look forward to.

Try your professional association, charitable foundations, special needs advocate organisations, alumni associations and local groups. An internet search of volunteer opportunities in your area of interest, say, for example "volunteer opportunities with animals near me" will identify a range of possibilities.

The assignments offered to new volunteers will usually be entry level and driven by need so don't expect to start at the top.

A volunteer assignment may be answering the phone, staffing a sales desk, making deliveries, dishing up food or serving on a committee. You will be reporting to someone else but may be expected to jump in and contribute with higher-level work. It's important to help willingly while understanding that organisations are initially looking for your time and effort.

To get the most out of volunteering, be willing to be open, flexible, and showcase leadership in whatever capacity you are working. After becoming involved you can start to navigate the organisation and identify different opportunities and roles that interest you.

When seeking volunteering assignments, ask yourself:

- Will it help me develop a new skill set or different perspective?
- What are the pathways to get to that position? Will I need to serve in other positions first?
- What skills do I need to develop and how can I develop them?

- Beyond the volunteer role, how will those skills help me in my work and career?

Some of the skills you could develop as a volunteer are: communication, persuasion, negotiation, project management, teamwork, and strategic planning.

Not only are you developing yourself for your professional life with the skills and attributes you gain as a volunteer, you are building competencies you can use in other roles and companies. You will be able to leverage volunteer experience to gain more skills and perspective and may even turn your volunteer role into your next job.

How to get the gig

There are many organisations and resources to help with finding a suitable volunteer role. There are several ways of finding trustee vacancies including looking on:

- Charity social media — it's a good idea to follow all those that inspire you
- Charity newsletters — sign up to all the charities in which you have an interest
- Local noticeboards or newspapers
- Local councils — check their websites for information
- Community Voluntary Services https://www.navca.org.uk/ where local charities and community groups come together
- Reach https://reachvolunteering.org.uk/recruit-volunteers is the UK's single biggest source of trustees for the voluntary sector.
- Charity Job https://www.charityjob.co.uk/ — an easy to use site advertising volunteering and paid charity roles.
- Peridot Partners https://www.peridotpartners.co.uk/boardmatch/ progressive and interesting trustee roles on an easy to use site, they recruit hundreds of trustees, chief executives and specialist directors to charities every year
- Trustees Unlimited https://trustees-unlimited.co.uk/ sign up for trustee position alerts
- Citizens Advice https://www.citizensadvice.org.uk/ volunteers from a range of backgrounds in a range of roles for local Citizens Advice and Witness Service

No matter where you choose to spend your volunteer time, it is important to find an organisation or cause that you can be passionate about. Networking is key to finding the right role with the right organisation.

Be realistic about the contribution you can make, alongside your work and personal commitments. People will be banking on your reliability and expect you take your responsibilities as an unpaid worker seriously. Consider a one-off event or short-term project if these might suit you better than a long-term commitment.

Strategically plan your volunteering

- Identify an organisation about which you are passionate. You will be using your free time, so make sure you care.

- Be willing to start in an entry-level role and bear in mind that the work probably won't be glamorous.
- Network with staff and other volunteers so that you connect not just with the cause but with others who are also committed to it.
- Develop the skills you need to be successful. Use the opportunity as a win-win and gain useful expertise.
- Re-evaluate yourself and your goals regularly to ensure the volunteering is giving you the skills and experience you hoped for and anticipated.
- Apply the knowledge you gain as a volunteer to your workplace and career as you grow and develop using your new skills in multiple situations.

Strategic volunteering helps you to learn more about the activities and fields you enjoy, identify strengths, build connections, and gain important skills and experiences. Volunteering may allow you to experience aspects or parts of an organisation with which you wouldn't necessarily interact otherwise.

Strategic volunteering may afford you valuable networking prospects, so many socially conscious individuals working toward a greater goal means volunteering allows opportunities to connect with like-minded people. It unites people from differing industries and backgrounds, which creates a unique network for volunteers, one completely unlike those you might develop in your own professional field.

Volunteering provides uncommon connections, and may lead to rare opportunities. Make it a priority to meet lots of people while volunteering; you never know who might be plugged in to connections and prospects that might interest you. All networking is useful.

Pitfalls

You may find you are using skills you no longer want to emphasise; it can be a bit of a busman's holiday. So, when I was briefly a governor for a Community College my driver was to increase the representation of ethnic minorities, but their requirement was for me was to sit in on grievance and disciplinary interviews, given my HR credentials. No foul, no harm but the situation wasn't sustainable as our aims weren't properly aligned.

Also, not for profits notoriously take up a huge amount of time. NHS trust board members and school governors will attest to this; they can seriously impact on your scheduling.

Key Takeaways from this chapter

Volunteering offers dual benefits: It's a rewarding way to give back while building new skills and expanding your network.

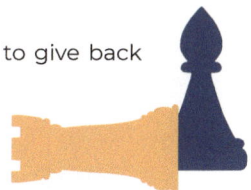

Chapter Thirteen

It's all about you

This chapter is dedicated to the final third of your portfolio career.

By this stage, you've established your remunerated work and found ways to give back. Now, it's time to embrace the freedom to, as Eddie and the Hot Rods famously put it,

"Do anything you want to do."

I'm not here to tell you how to approach this next chapter of your life — that's entirely up to you. Use this space to jot down your own bucket list. What excites you? What have you always dreamed of doing?

This is your moment to capture the ambitions, experiences and adventures that will bring this phase of your career to life. No limits, no rules — just your unique vision for what's next.

Enjoy the process.

What's Next? Write Your Own Adventure

Chapter Fourteen

Concluding thoughts:
Designing your future with a portfolio career

"Find a job you love, and you'll never work a day in your life."

This saying, attributed to luminaries from Confucius to Churchill, captures the essence of a portfolio career. This isn't just about multiple jobs or tasks — it's a journey towards crafting a life where your work genuinely reflects the real you.

A portfolio career offers liberation from the confines of traditional employment. It grants the freedom to dive into diverse ventures and be a more energised, well-rounded individual. The autonomy that comes with this approach can make you feel in command of your destiny, no longer tethered to one role or organisation.

That said, you do need to plan in advance. Think of your portfolio career as a marathon, not a sprint. The groundwork you lay before leaving your full-time job can be the difference between a smooth transition and a rocky start.

One thing this book has underscored repeatedly is the importance of lifelong learning. Learning should go beyond professional gains. Maybe learning Chinese won't land you a job with a Chinese business, but the intellectual fulfilment it provides will enrich your life. So, whether it's mastering a craft, learning a musical instrument or even earning an MBA, these aren't just nice-to-haves; they are testimony to your commitment to evolve and stay relevant.

Remember, market demands shift. The biggest risk to the portfolio career worker is a failure to invest in development, thus continuing to offer skills and expertise the marketplace no longer requires. Continual learning ensures you're not stuck offering obsolete skills. Predict where the industry is heading and stay ahead of the curve.

Your portfolio career's success is, in many ways, a blend of skills, interests, values and personality. While honing existing skills is crucial, foreseeing the future's requirements and preparing for them is equally vital. This forward-thinking approach, combined with robust networking and social skills, will set you apart.

But amid the hustle, never lose sight of what truly matters: joy. Regularly ask yourself: "Am I enjoying what I'm doing?" The beauty of a portfolio career is its adaptability. If a particular strand doesn't resonate with you any more, it's time to reassess and pivot.

In summary:

- Strategise: Plan meticulously but remain flexible to adjust and evolve
- Learn continuously: Embrace lifelong learning and stay attuned to market demands
- Network effectively: Cultivate connections and enhance your social skills
- Stay joyful: Regularly assess your happiness quotient and recalibrate if needed

I hope this book has encouraged you to embrace the journey of a portfolio career, where every venture is a new chapter, every skill acquired a new asset and every connection made a step closer to your dream. The world of work is filled with endless possibilities. So, take a deep breath, make that leap and craft the life you've always envisioned. The time to shape your unique portfolio is now. To quote Robin Williams:

"Carpe diem — seize the day".

Appendix One

Fuel50 is an AI-driven talent marketplace platform that fuels internal talent mobility, workforce agility, employee engagement, talent retention and bottom-line impact within leading organisations all over the world. The platform helps clients create career pathways and journeys within their organisation that match to the wants and needs of their people.

How to access Fuel50 to discover your personal values, career engagers and motivated talents:

Email info@10Eighty quoting the code PORTFOLIOCAREER and you will be given access to the questionnaires.

Appendix Two:
Our Stories

Our contributors

10Eighty fields a team of experienced, qualified and professional executive coaches, facilitators and leadership consultants who work with clients to build plans tailored to their organisation and goals. Our coaches are portfolio professionals and alongside their experience as coaches and mentors they work or have worked in professional services, financial services, the public sector, manufacturing, HR and marketing.

Our principles are straightforward:

- Everyone has potential and should have the opportunity to develop and realise that potential.
- We enable individuals to be comfortable and confident in taking ownership and responsibility for their actions and behaviours.
- Allowing everyone to operate independently and interdependently is a core element of our development programmes.
- We promote a strengths-based philosophy to enhance management and leadership capability and increase career resilience.
- The work we do should be of benefit to the individuals, organisations and communities we serve.
- Everything we do, we do with passion.

The 10Eighty executive coaches who contributed to this book provided insights from their own successful portfolio careers and from their work with our clients include:

Carol Ashton, David Bridges, Mike Grant, Chris Hale, Michaela Henshaw, Charles Hindson, Barry Joinson, Jeremy Leadsom, Michele Lahey, David Mellor, Paul Mussenden, Sue Mandelbaum, Mark Sismey-Durrant, Andrew Tallents and Tim Parrack. Charles Hindson's interview notes are not included at this request.

We talked to them about their portfolio careers, their motivation and the challenges they faced; we asked what they learned about themselves in the process and for their advice to readers. These interviews were carried out between February and May 2020.

David Bridges

After working at senior level for twenty odd years and contemplating the end of a full-time executive career, David decided he didn't want to retire at 52 but would rather work at a lower intensity for a longer time while seeking improved work-life balance.

A health scare prompted a rethink about what he wanted to do and what was important to him on all levels. He was a little bored of just doing the one thing and wanted a more peripatetic way of working and the variety involved in portfolio career. A few things combined to influence his decision to embark on a portfolio career.

How it worked out

He decided to pursue twin strands of non-executive director roles and consulting. In time he secured a non-executive director role and has established useful connections with chairmen in fields that interest him.

The consulting side was a success; he has good contacts and always worked hard at networking. His customers range from large to tiny, all from existing contacts, which he admits might be a worry for the future, but he has a strong network and maintains relationships with contacts. He suggests you need to be realistic and honest about the strength of your network, and clear about the state of the market and your own attractiveness, it pays to be focussed as circumstances will dictate your course of action; you must take your opportunities where they fall and be responsive.

He achieved a better work-life balance, not optimum because it was a strong learning curve, but in the first year he took more holiday than ever previously. The new lifestyle improved his family life, and he was less stressed. There were real positives, but it is important to ensure you book out time when you are going to be away or pursuing non-work projects.

On the administrative side, he had plenty of time to organise his business but managing the diary was the hardest aspect. His wife was involved with this. He says that keeping control of expenses can be hard for some people when they no longer have the support structure of an office behind them.

David made an unexpected comment;

" it was very interesting to see who stepped up to support and help, and the people I did not expect would help but who did so; and, conversely, some, a few, who just did not materialise. It was disappointing when they were people I had helped in the past, and there has been no quid pro quo".

David says *"I don't know what the future holds but that is quite exciting".*

Sometime after our interview, David took another full-time job, feeling that he still had a part to play in that specific role.

Michaela Henshaw

Michaela has been a portfolio careerist for some years because it links into her preferred lifestyle. She points out that what you envisage doesn't always pan out, you must be agile and resilient, able to think on your feet. It may take a period of time for you to establish a way of working that you are happy with, and sometimes things change as you go along, so be reasonable.

Michaela's advice

If a given project doesn't fit with your long-term plan and desired schedule then let it go; this is a different way of working, and you must think about your time and work in a different way. You are the only person who sees your 'big picture' in terms of what you enjoy doing and what you want your schedule to look like, so you need to take control — sometimes that means you have to say 'no'. You must learn to be particularly brave and say no if you don't have the time in your schedule for a piece of work that you find exciting.

Resilience is essential to perform at your best without compromising physical, mental and emotional wellbeing — we all want to be at our best so you need to organise yourself so that can happen in a consistent way.

The key driver is your energy level, so taking care of yourself is a priority. Think about what will help you maximise your energy levels — what can you do to drive your energy levels up? These will be a range of things from immediate energy boosts to more substantial energy givers in the medium and long term. Again, you need to learn when to say 'no', particularly if it will be stressful or does not align with your skills and aspirations.

Coping strategies involve clarity about what you are comfortable with and the things you are less familiar with. Don't be afraid to ask for help — who do you have in your network to help you with the new things you are dealing with, who can give you pointers and advice to navigate new fields and areas?

Planning is crucial, both in terms of work and free time; if you are based from home you have to create a boundary between work and home, put steps in place to protect your 'me' time. Not just planning for the next day or next week but a year in advance; have a rolling plan and forecast for work and leisure so you can fit work around it, otherwise you end up saying yes to everything and never get a holiday.

Remember your schedule has to constantly build in networking time so you don't neglect your future pipeline of business.

There is no substitute for making a detailed plan around expectations and outcomes when agreeing to piece of work; pin down the timescale the client is working to, and before you commit ensure you do enough planning to see if it is realistic. Sometimes you have to be brave about pointing out that if a specific outcome is required then the timescale may have to be adjusted, or the output adjusted. Seek to map out timings and outputs and be clear that time is blocked out, so you don't oversell.

Michele Lahey

Michele combines career coaching with her consultancy contract with a university. She has been working for them for some time; what started as a six-month project has morphed and extended — she is flying all over place to undertake a review of training and the quality of nursing and is also involved in implementing recommendations.

She set up a business consultancy because she really enjoys working with people and says the market is right for people at later career stages who have had success and want to keep on contributing but by doing different things.

What Michele learned

Support can be an issue if you are not necessarily equipped to work with IT or with spreadsheets. Overall, she is organised about administration and following through, but not really good at selling — it is not a natural thing for her, and she says she is in awe of more sophisticated networkers.

On networking, Michele says mostly her expectations of people were consistent with what then happened.

> *"Generally speaking, I have found people gracious and willing to meet, some are more helpful than others, and there was no negative push back".*

Your network knows you, know your work and have faith in you and trust you to do what you say you will do.

The fundamental thing is to do work that you really love, so you are involved with something you care about, contributing to the greater good or whatever; it is a joy, though not always easy, but that makes for a rewarding experience.

If you want to sit on a charity board, find something that is important to you, something where you can make a difference. Michele has loved every minute of her career; she never set out to be a CEO but has been privileged to work on things she felt passionate about and imagining the possibilities is great fun.

Chris Hale

Chris has been a lawyer for 40 years and was senior partner of the law firm at which he spent most of his career. After standing down he has remained as a consultant, initially for three days a week reducing to one day a week from 1 July 2021. In the meantime, he has been building up a portfolio of other activities.

- Education — lecturing, writing and governor of a school
- Voluntary sector — trustee of two charities involved in the field of justice and one associated with his legal practice area: private equity
- Business — member of an angel network, adviser to two businesses and looking for chair role in a private equity business

He spoke to a number of people about portfolio work and his guiding principle is doing what he enjoys, where he can do things in different areas that have interested him and whereby he can give something back with a focus on others rather than himself.

Chris has always had a connection with the academic world and has good contacts there so networking has been important, but people have been unexpectedly helpful. He has been surprised by how willing people are to give their time and make introductions.

Learning points

He has learned that he is not very good at sitting around not doing much. He needs to stimulate and engage his mind, and it is essential that he takes care of his wellbeing; he discovered that he is forward rather than backward looking, optimistic and energetic and engaged about the future.

He doesn't worry if a plan does not pan out exactly; he has good contacts and realises that in current circumstances that things may change, and other things will come along. Realistically he will have to adapt and change with the situation.

His advice is to think about what you want to do after you leave what has been your main occupation sooner rather than later, get advice from others who have been on this journey and get some perspective — a coach or mentor to help crystallise thoughts and put your plans in a structured context. As a start he suggests working out what you want out of the next phase of life — intellectual stimulation, remuneration, time to do something different with your life, and whether you want to work full-time or part-time.

Paul Mussenden

Paul's portfolio is still evolving. He obtained his first non-executive role (at a healthcare charity) while still working in a full-time role and enjoyed the diversity of work that provided.

After leaving full-time employment when his employer was acquired by another company, he decided expansion of his portfolio would be an ideal way to exploit his varied skills and provide a different way of working, having been at the one organisation for 19 years in a variety of roles.

He was very deliberate about what he wanted and was explicit with others that he was not looking for a job but was interested in consultancy/NED work, specifically in the healthcare sector. Clarity around his aims meant the courting phase was easier, though it would often take 3-4 months or more to establish whether the fit and timing were right for both parties.

He was headhunted to the unpaid charity role which complemented his existing experience of working with diverse boards and helped him position himself as a non-executive director and opened doors to other potential roles.

His portfolio originally consisted of being Deputy Chairman and Chair of the Audit Committee at a leading life science charity. He currently holds two non-executive roles at a Canadian public healthcare fund and at two privately owned healthtech companies. Those roles were attained via networking and third-party contacts. He has since transitioned from a non-executive to the CEO role at one of the healthtech companies.

He ultimately envisages returning to a purely portfolio role. He found the challenge of non-executive roles enjoyable as he was using his experience to assist other companies at various stages of development but also having to consider how to translate that in new areas and for new businesses, each with their own challenges and opportunities.

Moving from an executive role into the NED space has brought tremendous opportunities, and he sought out roles at smaller tech companies where his experience of larger growing businesses and corporate transactions were particularly valued.

How it worked out

He surprised himself by enjoying the networking, as there was no pressure to find a job, and by being really open minded and patient some interesting opportunities presented themselves.

The portfolio option isn't the easy option, but he wanted diversity and a bit more time to himself and to try to find the right balance. It can be quite full on at times and an important role is working effectively with the rest of the board and management team to drive the right discussions and outcomes. It can suck up all your time, so you must be quite disciplined.

There is merit in exploring new areas but having started his career as a scientist he wanted to do something purposeful, so for him that involves the healthcare and tech field. His motive is feeling he is helping build a company and mentoring the people and teams, doing something purposeful in healthcare area.

Going forward

Some people manage a good balance of work, giving back through charitable roles and personal time though Paul feels that probably he has allowed that third bit to be a poor relation.

Paul pursued portfolio working deliberately but originally said he would consider a full-time role if the right job cropped up where he could really add value and help build a company. That is subsequently exactly what happened with Paul taking the CEO role while continuing a few non-executive roles.

Paul's advice

Be patient. My networking skills have improved exponentially, and my understanding of the market has also grown hugely.

Each company board and culture is different and you can't assume that what worked elsewhere will work everywhere although, of course, there are common principles of good practice, effective communication, ensuring effective decision making, combined in a way that is practical which works differently in each situation. Many NED jobs require more than expertise; they want your networking skills and for you to open doors for them, intangible stuff over and above job experience; they want to know that you will be an enabler and facilitator on the board, that you offer a broader skillset and perspective.

The ability to help influence and facilitate an effective board culture and engagement is very valuable, as well as problem solving. Ultimately being a trusted advisor and providing a sounding board for the executive in a mentoring role is something that I really enjoy, for example, helping them understand the mindset of the board.

*"Be opportunistic; things may come at the wrong time
but take your chances where you find them."*

David Mellor

Be prepared for the unexpected — the proportion of people finding fulfilment with a portfolio career based on what they had in mind when starting out is only around 30% — so manage your expectations.

"I am not doing what I expected when I set out"
David is a business school lecturer and executive, which is not the
portfolio he originally envisaged

He says it's a kind of Darwinian concept — adapt and survive, you have to have the courage to admit when things don't work, maybe just because of bad timing, or the market may decide it needs something different to what you chose to sell, or maybe you just had the right idea at the wrong time.

Be prepared to flex and think more broadly. You may not have to change your ideas but simply flex the way things work; aim to provide a solution to a problem rather than looking for problems to solve. Do your research to be sure that the fish will bite, that people need what you offer.

Try to find out what people want, in terms of roles and how to secure the roles you want. So, how do you break into new areas? The most successful people are those who decided to go part-time doing something for which they were known and that kind of them helps them fund research into other interests and pro bono work.

The most common portfolio mix is doing 'something I know alongside something I always wanted to, as well as giving something back'. Try to tease out what it is that really floats your boat!

David says that self-awareness is crucial. Take a serious look at whether you have really got what it takes; you may be a subject matter expert but that doesn't mean you are a business person. Many people are not good at figures or selling, so understanding the drivers behind your decisions is important and you will need a level of business acumen.

Coming out of a big organisation means you are, to some extent, institutionalised, and becoming a business person is a challenge, selling your own service is a different matter to selling your house or car.

Assuming you are well prepped, and have portfolio that makes sense, bear in mind that various components take off at different speeds and one can strangle others. You have to cope with that; you will realise you are successful when different parts of the portfolio are competing for your time.

There is a lot to do around time management because you don't want to chase everything and exhaust yourself — be a sniper, not a blunderbuss and pick the right opportunities in the right sectors.

In terms of networking, quality of contacts is more important than the size of your network. David started from scratch with building a new network, going to events and forums, at most of which he found more vultures than carcasses, people who wanted to sell to him rather than hearing what he had to offer. He learned from it and decided to invest time and energy in a select group of contacts.

Look at your contacts through three filters:

- For how many do you have 100% mutual trust and respect?
- With how many of them do you have a genuine reciprocal relationship?
- For how many are you safe in the knowledge they are always reliable?

That gives a core network to rely on and David says 100% of new business has come from that group, and that they are trusted colleagues.

Without over-analysing have a way to measure how your different income streams are doing, so you can take stock and have a long hard look at the mix and see what works and ease out of something that doesn't repay effort; then if something comes up you are not expecting you can take on interesting work as it arises without conflict.

Mike Grant

Mike is an Executive Coach, who focuses on leadership and team coaching as well as some facilitation. He also holds a Master's in Integrative Psychotherapy and has a Psychotherapy private practice alongside his executive coaching practice.

He previously had a successful career within financial services but wanted to find a new direction as he felt the environment wasn't particularly healthy for him. He says that when he began to think about what he would like to do, it was interesting that someone who, on the face of it, had everything going for him and was good at what he did, he no longer enjoyed it!

With an interest in psychotherapy, he undertook a master's in executive Coaching with Ashridge Business School, that was sympathetic to the psychotherapy approach he wanted to take. With the master's degree under his belt he then started his Executive Coaching practice.

In the early days of his practice, Mike says he tried some things he did not enjoy — training and working in the Middle East with a financial services client, as well as some web marketing seminars, but felt they didn't align with his aspirations.

Executive Coaching, however, was successful quite quickly in part, due to his strong network and good reputation. He reached out to his network and received introductions and referrals that brought him interesting work. He also ensured he built relationships with consultancies and other coaches.

In terms of networking Mike believes that if you put in enough work on leads, results will come. Good relationships need nurturing. The big surprise is that it is sometimes easier than you would think, the idea of asking for work can be difficult for some, but Mike never really saw it that way — sales is about communications and building rapport.

Mike was fortunate that, after he left his senior role of 30 years within financial services, he was able to take time to build his practice. With hindsight he probably would not have done the training because what he really enjoys is the one to one work and real engagement with clients.

Key advice

"Having been an employee I initially doubted that I would be able to build my practice and be self-employed, but along the way I learned a lot about myself about my own resourcefulness. I learned to enjoy the flexibility it gave me and learned to enjoy free time and the wider variety of work I do now and the people I meet. I love the change of pace, the gaps when I have time to think, and people watch."

His advice would be to think about what you really want and what motivates you — the grass is not always greener. Consider what your USP is — what sets you apart from other coaches — how are you different and why would someone want to engage you as their coach. Then define this and show how it fits with what you want to do.

Think about your network — You need a good network, a good core of people who will help you, what does your network look like, do you have enough connections.

Mike commented that whilst he initially worried that he would not get work, his practice is now strong, and he is more relaxed. He adds

"It creates freedom for me. There is nothing I miss about the corporate world. I find being in institutions quite disruptive."

Carol Ashton

As a senior HR professional working in a large global law firm, she says it was exhausting and draining, tough and sometimes lonely. She was on a treadmill and always running with little no time to stop and think about her future and her own career plan. Carol knew it was about time for change, but change would mean a new role and she was too busy to look up and look around for opportunities.

Personal circumstances and illness in the family, made it even harder to create the headspace to decide what she wanted, and look around; then she was brought up short by a redundancy conversation. As the HR leader she had, of course, seen the decision coming, but was surprised by the timing.

Dusting off her CV Carol started talking to head-hunters, but with the benefit of an 'enforced sabbatical' realised she was at a stage in her life and career where a new role would mean another much the same as the role she was leaving, with the same issues, politics and relentless pressure and frankly that was no longer attractive, not what she really wanted. Also, some of the interviews she attended left her feeling low in energy and this caused her to stop and reflect on why that was.

On the personal front, with her husband seriously ill, it meant she needed to be there more for him going forward, with less time on the road and at work. She was working long hours with a long commute and overseas travel, so her personal situation caused a rethink around continuing her career in a different but more fulfilling and more flexible way.

In exploring her options, Carol says she had coffee with anybody who would meet up with her. She notes that people were extremely generous with their time and their advice — she got lots of tips and notably nobody she spoke to regretted making the transition to a portfolio career, albeit they also gave health warnings about losing corporate support, the risk of loneliness, peaks and troughs in workload and financial security, and the chaos that diary management can become!

How it played out

Eventually she had to get off the fence — and is now working independently from her home office, about an hour commute out of London, so must be quite disciplined in planning her diary to make sure days in London are well used.

Her service offering is executive coaching and HR consulting either in support roles or on a retained basis for small organisations, and those that need back-up, perhaps on specific projects such as training programmes, or for SMEs who do not have full-fledged recruitment function but have issues where they need the input of an HR professional.

Interim work was not intended to be part of her portfolio, however in the early days she did take on a contract as the opportunity was good, in a company she respected, and she was able to negotiate part-time hours which allowed the advantage of providing cashflow while building out the broader portfolio of work.

Turning work down is a dilemma but if you either don't have capacity or the role does not hit your sweet spot, then recognise you would probably not deliver your best work. You are going to have to say 'no' to someone at some time — and your reputation with the client is better preserved by introducing them to someone who will do a great job for them — while in the meantime leaving you free to take up projects that are more aligned to your experience and interest. This, of course, can work in the other direction too, and Carol has been happy to take on work that was referred to her by contacts who were not available/not right for a particular job.

Carol says that averaged over the year she probably is working fewer hours, however, one big learning point — it is not straightforward as, at times, she is probably working more hours and that means business development effort can slip.

Making time for networking is very important as she is independent, clients are buying her expertise and that is very much driven by her network. Her working principle is what powers those relationships is her, so maintaining her network is an important part of what show she spends her time. A surprise was that a lot of fruitful relationships are new ones, which is good, and has enabled her to spread her wings in to other industries other than professional services where she spend most of her corporate career. No referral or personal introduction has ever resulted in a wasted conversation. Much of her new work comes from second level network connections.

Work did come from sources that surprised her, including some work from virtual strangers, people she had known for a matter of hours, and from a head-hunter with whom she explored non-executive director opportunities but who introduced her to contacts for coaching, and HR consulting work.

She initially envisaged taking a non-executive directorship into her portfolio for a few days per year and fit in with coaching or consulting projects, and was asked to apply for trustee roles, one for a chair she knows and respects and one for an organisation that she wants to work for. This area is still a work in progress

Head-hunters have been very helpful in terms of general advice and personal introductions but it's worth remembering that most of their work is quite transactional and role-specific, and so you shouldn't realistically expect them to keep in touch.

Her advice is not to worry so much around defining a USP, building a website, or drafting a profile; she says live in it for a while first, then you will know what you want. What works comes from doing the work, and going with the flow, it is sometimes less than perfect, and you will make mistakes but go with it.

Carol says if you think you want do this, think about it when still in paid employment — if you can secure a non-executive director role while in employment, with permission from your employer, or cultivate your network so it aids your readiness for the change. If in doubt take the leap, give it a try!

It is quite important to put a timeline on it, dive in but set a limit to review and check in — is this working well, or do I need Plan B? Treat your portfolio career like any other project and be realistic.

It is very easy to focus on your new portfolio work and not take time for yourself; you need not to overwhelm yourself because you don't have the definition of the office anymore.

Carol says she doing all her own administration, mainly because she is a control freak, but she has an accountant as she knows her strengths and detail and numbers are not her forte; the other area is IT where she has someone to call on who helped set up her systems, diary management and admin.

Moving forward

Carol found the pandemic and the various lockdowns very scary for someone who had recently moved to a way of working that does not bring a monthly predictable salary. It also highlighted even further the need to define the boundaries between work and home. On the plus side, it presented different opportunities to explore video-based coaching relationships, virtual networking and afforded time and space to pursue professional development such as team coaching.

Her portfolio has now been rounded out with two Board committee roles and a new NED position.

Andrew Tallents
Building a Successful NED Career

We talked to Andrew specifically about the non-executive directorship option. His first piece of advice is to ask yourself: why do you want to be a non-executive director? Too often recently retired leaders are given the advice that this is an option, they then feel flattered and start looking for a non-executive director role.

That's not a good reason to do it. You need to know and understand yourself; do you feel it is time to give something back? Rather than leading and doing this is about giving back by making a different sort of contribution. So be clear about your reasons and purpose and why that is a fit for a non-executive director role when you are being interviewed as you will come across as more authentic and convincing.

It also partly depends on what you do now, so once you have the right reason, then decide what kind of non-executive do I want to be and therefore which type of board should I join? This is about self-leadership, about your own contribution and making a good fit, as opposed to applying for roles as they come up. Self-direction is important.

What kind of chair do you want to work with?

Once you have those elements sorted then you need to be proactive in your own network and tell people what you are looking for.

Some people are unrealistic about the likelihood of obtaining a non-executive director role but there are also many who under-estimate their ability to get such a role. You do need to have the right background and skills, so be realistic, but manage your search and see what happens.

What does a chair want?

- Curiosity. You have got to be interested in how the business is being run.
- Emotional intelligence, can you manage relationships with executives.
- The ability to hold others to account which can come from executive experience but not too many executives do, in fact, hold their teams to account.
- The ability to hold back, in a way, till your contribution is required; quality not quantity is an issue'. You need to be able to pay attention, listen, observe, absorb a lot of information until it is time to ask the CEO the one question that makes him stop and think, the question that will make a real difference to the approach taken or the direction of travel. So listening and understanding are key.

Potential non-executive directors don't always understand how much work is involved, and the legal obligations they will be undertaking. If you are currently in an executive role and looking for a first non-executive director role or have several non-executive director roles already, be sure to have written in formally the number of days you are able to commit to a non-executive director role; it seems to be always underestimated, be realistic.

Barry Joinson

Barry says that in terms of lifestyle considerations you should think about:

Recognising what you need and what works for you, what is realistic for you?

What is your attitude to risk? Your financial security threshold? A variable income can be stressful; think about pensions, health insurance, critical illness cover.

Be realistic — you won't have a guaranteed salary or pension contribution or holiday allowance but nor will you have a boss other than yourself AND you won't have an office or office support, watercooler moments and back-up!

Doing something with meaning and purpose, something where you can make a difference, perhaps including a better work/life balance. If you prefer variety, or love learning, or doing something different a portfolio career can be aligned with your values.

Doing something with meaning and purpose was fundamental to making the change; Barry felt he was no longer adding value. He wanted to make a positive impact and did not feel he was doing that anymore. However, finding his purpose was quite challenging as he had a sense of what he wanted to do but not how to articulate it.

For Barry there was a piece about finding help to crystallise the aspiration and enable him to do something that reflected how he wanted his life to be. He was conscious that he could go and get another job in the city like the one he was leaving but would not necessarily be able to get that sort of salary if he worked for himself.

So there had been something else for him — time to spend with family, to study, to read and do things that worked for him that meant something real to him. Barry says a lot of people forget the 'me' part and end up setting up something that is too like what they had before; the advantage of a portfolio career is working on projects that are meaningful and that align with your passion.

He relishes the variety, using skills and knowledge through various means, coaching, supervision, writing and encourages people not to think that a job title defines what you are.

The higher you climb the less interesting the work becomes for some of us, you are doing more of the strategic thinking and less of the actual 'doing' and that was less appealing to Barry. He says it is about balance and if you love your work, it is often not really work, he feels like the luckiest person on the planet, as now work is about what can he do today that will make a difference.

Portfolio working is likely to mean a variable income; you still have to pay for all the things you need, and things you perhaps used to take for granted are no longer there, so you have to find time and energy to deal with that and put those things in place. He suggests you take help where you need it — he outsourced the accounting and administration.

Key advice:

The key is to plan, plan, and plan again. Think about the people you spend your life with and how your change of direction impacts them, you are likely to be relying on family more for support including emotional and psychological support. You will no longer have a peer group to refer to, so that may mean a big change at home, it puts pressure on the people around you, the power dynamic changes.

Your business starts and ends with you so if you are sick, you don't generate income; have you got sufficient funds to cover yourself? You also must think about making best use of your resources and managing your invoicing and income as well as managing the pipeline of work.

When you are working you are not developing the business, so you need to charge enough to cover the lulls, consider how much your time is worth to you as well as what the work is worth to the client, are you charging for preparation time?

You may find ways to passively grow the business either with a network of referrers, or by outsourcing social media for instance. Pick your networks wisely, he started with scattergun approach, but it is better to target your audience, be clear about your niche.

It is about who you know — reach out to people your target audience have a relationship with, it's much easier than trying to approach someone cold.

He says a good place to build business is on training courses, seminars and things like that, where there are other people like you hanging out. He has built good relationships and got work that way, valuable business came via that route.

Don't underestimate the time it takes to build your network, people you already know may not give you work once you are an independent. You have to be a credible resource, and it can take months to get clearance for a project and then months more to get paid.

If you are a parent or carer with responsibilities you need to adapt, make sure you arrange work to fit in all the other things you have on the go; you may need to put a lot of focus on the business when you first start out.

Know your strengths: if you are not good at selling and pitching for business then you will struggle to grow the business. Most business is created through people you know, but bear in mind that, depending on your line of business, there may be conflicts of interest to deal with.

"

An accountability buddy who will hold your feet to the fire can be invaluable.

"

Initially Barry took everything offered but then learned that some kinds of work will do nothing but tear out your heart and leave you with a bad reputation, so the sooner you learn to turn down work that you don't want to do the better; most clients will appreciate it if you explain why.

Sometimes people feel that they have never been able to do things the way they really wanted and that, as an independent, they will be able to things properly and put the world to rights, but it doesn't really work that way. The client still wants what the client wants and often it is not 'proper' and that can be hard to come to terms with.

Recognising your successes is important, acknowledge when things are going well and reward yourself liberally because there will be plenty of times when you feel things are not going well, so you need a balance.

Be realistic about what motivates you but if you are intuitive and work well in a freeform environment you probably don't need a step by step plan, relish the freedom to make the business what you want it to be, acknowledge that some of the work is low paid and maybe some is high paid, that is fine, see it in the round.

Be realistic about how much money you really need — a wonderful benefit of this way of working is that you can ramp it up and then take two months off, you need to find a balance as overheads and costs carry on even if you don't.

An accountability buddy who will hold your feet to the fire can be invaluable. It is useful to pick someone with a different approach, so you offer one another assistance; don't rely on people who are too like you, you need a diverse range of people around you.

Be careful of becoming a guru — if you are the brightest person the room you are in the wrong room!

In terms of pride and ego it can be difficult to leave your smart office, and the next day feel you are invisible so it is important to have social and professional support group around you, get out and see people, make yourself visible.

A level of pragmatism is required, you are more dispensable, so think about who you are meeting on the way up as you may meet them on the way down.

Relationships are everything, across the whole range of your concerns, which is a massive opportunity!

Jeremy Leadsom

Runs a portfolio career comprising non-executive directorships, charity work, fly fishing and walking. After 12 years in the Army, Jeremy spent 28 years in asset management in London on the sales/marketing side, the last 20 years for same organisation. He wanted to do other things whilst he still had excess energy. He wanted to work part-time, half of which should be paid. He was motivated by doing some unpaid stuff.

He is a Chair at a Brighton based prisoners' families charity (which converted from a community interest company last year, 2024), a non-executive director at an IFA and a role as a board advisor to a small asset management company. He feels he is on track with his aspirations.

As an IFA NED, as well as governance he provides some sensible sales and marketing advice and that, inevitably, feels a bit like consulting. He is still looking to add some more mentoring which he did previously and enjoyed far more than he ever expected.

Think about your mental health and engagement, as anyone planning a portfolio career, coming out of a high contact, intense environment and stepping back will find the impact of the change needs to be managed.

He is trying to build his portfolio as he is not as occupied as he wants to be, wants to be busier in winter and less busy in the other half of the year; it requires self-discipline and mentoring was very helpful.

Networking is a never stop activity, there is more focus on networking in this sort of life, use your contacts as eyes and ears; most weeks he plans networking activity.

Some of his best connections, people known for a very long time, have been the least forthcoming, less useful than expected, others have been more useful.

He told his employer three years before he left, so they could do succession planning, which worked well. Jeremy knew what he wanted to do but was not entirely sure how to execute it, he spoke to friends and got a lot of advice: half advised him to switch off and do something completely different, but that was not for right for him.

The variety is great, a range of things on the go, and the one he gets most buzz from is a charity which is trying to diversify its income stream, helping them put together a pitch book to articulate what they do to potential investors.

Key advice:

Have a plan, take some time out, really try to identify honestly what you are good at and enjoy and be sure you have confidence in that. Check with others that they are seeing the same, then look at how best you articulate that to others — can I add value, do I believe in what I am doing, am I going to have fun? It's more important to spend time with the right people than being in 'the right' place.

You may miss the day to day cut and thrust, the daily banter, support in facing challenges; it can feel a little isolated, you don't have the level of support you get in a big corporation. But he likes working closely with small teams, the people at the charity are quite different, and he is learning a lot there.

"What makes it fun and worthwhile is ultimately if I can add value, and can see it, otherwise I won't be at my best"

A mentor is invaluable, when you decide you want to do this. There is lots of advice out there, but some membership groups want a subscription or membership fee and his advice would be rely on your network and ensure technical, tactical stuff is in place — don't pay out unnecessarily for things that probably won't help.

Sue Mandelbaum

Sue's portfolio is a mixed diet: she is a consultant advising professional services firms, is a coach and a magistrate, school governor and a trustee to two charities and a member of an HRA research ethics committee.

When last employed, Sue had already been trustee of a charity for several years, and knew she wanted to do more of that, she actively wanted to create a fairly varied life. Sue wanted to work and earn but also to actively participate in civil society and to be socially aware as she knew she got a huge amount from those activities.

Key advice:

Think about the things you are interested in and whether you can develop the relevant skills along the way. For example, if you want a trustee role and have not had any relevant responsibility then start to work on that, for example getting involved in management or leadership roles or getting involved in task-forces to develop the skills you need; do what you can to get started by way of small roles which you can run alongside your professional life.

In making the change to broaden out into a portfolio career you will find your pathway evolves over time and networking is critical. Treat networking as a campaign to chat to people who may be useful. It is worthwhile to network in systematic way and put together a spreadsheet to keep track of contacts.

You never know which conversations will be useful, and Sue's experience is that some interesting roles have come about from unlikely initial conversations. It may be from people known for years; most are generally open and positive, and both paid work and pro bono work have come from meetings which might not have appeared promising.

Learning as you go

Sue learned she is a lot more dogged and tenacious than she thought and better at marketing too; she is organised, robust, good at getting out there, sticking with things, can innovate more than she thought and has created consulting offerings that she had not thought about until a chance conversation spurred her on.

She says that reviewing where she is, she feels incredibly lucky to have the things she does and which she enjoys so much. She has a new perspective and feels that working with motivated people is a privilege.

Sue advises you to work out what is important — reflect on your whole life, what you like and what interests you, identify the threads you may pick up and develop. Examine in detail your career timeline to work out where to go next and shape something that suits you.

Be honest about yourself and what you can contribute. Planning ahead is important but be flexible and adaptable, don't think this is exactly what I want as that is bound to lead to disappointment.

Things don't always work out: think about resilience and mental health, stepping away from the structures of professional life can be difficult, so consider the support you might get, and where that will come from.

You may be able to rely on a mentor, for instance, so you have something that replaces the office support and gives you a sounding board, which is useful. A good idea is to build yourself a personal board with a group of people you can assemble to advise and support you.

Using an accountant is sensible, and Sue has a virtual assistant but rarely uses her. She tries to keep things as simple as possible but if you have a complicated life, you may need more help. It is important to have boundaries, build in exercise and time for yourself.

Mark Sismey-Durrant

Mark says his main advice to people thinking about a portfolio career is to start planning early; a lot depends on your seniority in an organisation and whether you will be allowed to do something beyond your normal day job that does not conflict with your paid role.

He was asked to stand for election as President of the Alumni Association at Loughborough University and because of that was also appointed as a Lay member of the University Council. After his three-year term as President, he was asked to Chair the University Audit Committee for six years, continuing throughout as a Member of Council and serving as a Pro-Chancellor. He says it was a great learning experience and he loved every minute of it. He is still involved as Chair of the Strategic Advisory Board of Loughborough Business School.

He has served on the Board of the BBA and UK Finance and chaired the Audit and Oversight Committee for UK Finance. For a number of years, he chaired both trade associations specialist/smaller banks Advisory Boards.

He has been a trustee of several charities and serves on the Development Board for the creative arts charity Create and as a trustee for the Bedford School Foundation Trust. He is a Freeman, Liveryman and Council Member for the Worshipful Company of International Bankers and served as Master in 2018/19. He chaired its Charity and Educational Committee for several years. Much of this work goes on in the evening. He has also served as Chair of the British Icelandic Chamber of Commerce.

He has served as Chairman of two dual regulated UK banks, as SID and Chair of Risk Committee for another AIM listed UK Bank. He has also chaired an AIM listed specialist lender, a privately owned lender and a Swedish Finance business. All these roles have called for a deep technical understanding of the regulatory environment and corporate governance more generally.

A lot of people don't really understand the extent of the governance involved in such roles, but this is critical to guide what the organisation is trying to do and how you can help.

Do your networking well in advance of when you need help. Networking is always best done when there is no immediate ulterior motive. Mark says roles have always found him and that happens because he is out and about, talking to people and helping them. Use networking to showcase what you can contribute without having to do it.

It is hardest to get your first non-executive directorship as there is the obvious barrier in that you have no experience! Becoming a trustee of a charity or in other areas where the main purpose is governance, perhaps where you are effectively a poacher turned gamekeeper, gives you the chance to try something different and develop your skills and experience.

Roles come because someone is looking to fill a need, you must be sure of the people you are working with; we sometimes can tend not to look at things from the other persons perspective and that can lead to surprises!

Mark says when he was first made redundant from his first CEO role, he found he knew loads of people but when he needed to chat with them realised they were mates and not really able to help with jobs. He made a vow to himself to always accept an approach from others when he was back in a CEO role — remembering how hard it was to get to the right contacts.

He had not really planned for redundancy and says from a self-esteem perspective continuing to be 'somebody' was quite important at that time. Since then he went on to take on two further CEO roles and he has set up two consultancy businesses which helped with this.

Not having financial commitments makes you more open-minded about what you can do, handling interim roles on a professional basis require you to be clear about where most time needs to be spent.

Think about taking care of yourself — health and work life balance and family time — when he stopped, he had to make adjustments and give himself permission to do stuff that was not work. The transition has come about gradually, Mark probably has more things in his portfolio than he would like but people he likes and respects have asked him to do things.

He says he has slowed down his speed reading, and thinks he now reads more deeply and takes on more detail, so knows he reads more carefully.

The other thing which is a huge benefit is walking the dogs. It is when Mark solves problems, and he wishes he had had more time as a chief executive to spend time thinking about things!

Don't over-think and unless you have a burning ambition to do something be open to the opportunities. Mark found lots of projects came along that he would not have designed into his plan, but things have fallen into place.

He learned that some working habits die hard, he is working as hard as ever; the fact that people ask him to do things is great, he thought he would be in full control but if you are naturally curious then you have conversations that open new vistas.

He doesn't really farm much out; he has an accountant; a virtual assistant would be helpful but you need enough work to pay for it. He needed to get organised first, keeping on top of technology is a nightmare, and bear in mind that if you become involved with a regulated business there is a lot of security around email accounts which can take a lot of time.

Tim Parrack

Tim is a Director at The Marketing Centre, an organisation that provides around 100 senior-level, part-time marketing directors — also known as Fractional CMOs — to ambitious businesses across the South East.

The Marketing Centre specialises in recruiting experienced portfolio professionals. Ideal candidates typically have a strong corporate background, a solid reputation in the industry, and around 20 years of top-level marketing experience. All hold degrees, many have MBAs, and usually have at least some prior consulting experience.

Tim feels that corporate marketing can be demanding and often undervalued. Many marketers reach their mid-40s or 50s and start to seek a better work-life balance beyond the corporate grind. An experienced top-level marketer will have extensive, transferable skills, but working independently as a consultant can be challenging. As a sole operator, you're responsible for personal success, staying current in the industry, and managing all aspects of your business. The lack of support can make this transition difficult for many as they build their portfolio of businesses.

The Marketing Centre addresses this challenge by offering a strong support system that most independent consultants lack. Through knowledge sharing, idea exchange, and collaborative experiences, it provides a valuable network. While some members are highly experienced consultants, most benefit significantly from having this kind of support system in place. Consulting experience, while beneficial, is not essential. As part-time marketing directors, professionals at The Marketing Centre focus on client strategy while the organisation handles administrative and business development tasks, allowing them to concentrate on delivering impactful marketing solutions.

This career path suits professionals of all ages. Some younger executives who climb the corporate ladder quickly may find themselves seeking alternative paths earlier in their careers. However, portfolio careers typically appeal to more seasoned professionals who can manage their workload at a comfortable pace.

The primary motivation for this transition is often the desire for a proactive change in work-life balance. While some professionals turn to consulting out of necessity after leaving corporate roles, Tim feels that the more successful ones are those who have chosen it deliberately as a new career direction.

He highlights that The Marketing Centre offers opportunities beyond just pure financial reward. However, the recruitment process is rigorous, as the organisation only selects top-tier professionals. He advises those entering consulting to leverage their networks, as personal connections often yield the best results.

The Marketing Centre primarily works with businesses that have grown entrepreneurially and reached a stage where their initial strategies are no longer sufficient to maintain a steady level of growth. At this point, they require a seasoned marketing specialist to align their marketing efforts with business objectives.

Additionally, second-generation-led businesses often seek The Marketing Centre's expertise to strengthen their marketing capabilities.

These companies are typically faced with a choice between a mid-level marketer, who may well be capable but is likely to be strategically limited, or engage a part-time marketing director from The Marketing Centre — not as a temporary fix, but as an ongoing strategic commitment. The average tenure for a marketing director in this model exceeds 12 months and often extends for several years. Establishing long-term value in any business engagement is crucial.

Success in this role requires the right mindset. Those heavily reliant on corporate structures and extensive internal support may find independent consulting challenging. However, professionals with a consultative mindset and strong influencing skills thrive in this environment.

Tim acknowledges that portfolio work isn't for everyone — it demands effort, self-motivation, and strong business development skills. Before making the transition, professionals need to be honest with themselves: do they possess or can they develop the necessary attributes to succeed?

References

Benko, Cathleen, *The Corporate Lattice: Achieving High Performance In The Changing World of Work*, Harvard Business Review Press, 2010

Clark, Dorie, *Entrepreneurial You: Monetize Your Expertise, Create Multiple Income Streams, and Thrive,* Harvard Business Review Press, 2017

Irene Mandi, *Eurofound Research, New Form of Employment 2020*

Gladwell, Malcolm, *The Tipping Point, How Little Things Can Make a Big Difference,* Abacus

Gratton, L. and Scott, A., *The Hundred Year Life: Living and Working in an Age of Longevity,* Bloomsbury Information, 2016

Greenspan, Michael, *How to Launch a Successful Portfolio Career,* The Harvard Business Review, 2017

Handy, Charles, *The Age of Unreason: New Thinking for a New World,* Random House Business, 2002,

Handy, Charles, *The Elephant and the Flea: New Thinking for a New World* Random House Business

Hoffman, Reid, *The Alliance: Managing Talent in the Networked Age*, Harvard Business Review Press, 2014

IPSE, *Making the Case for Freelancers,* www.ipse.co.uk/campaigns/other-campaigns/making-the-case-for-freelancers-report

Mandl, I, *Eurofound, New forms of employment, 2020 update,* 2020, eurofound.europa.eu/en/publications/2020/new-forms-employment-2020-update

Mirvis, P. H., & Hall, D. T. *Psychological success and the boundaryless career. Journal of Organizational Behaviour,* 1994

Moran, Michael, *The Guide to Everlasting Employability,* Lulu.com, 2012

Peiperl, M. and Baruch, Y., *Back to Square Zero: The Post-Corporate Career* Organizational Dynamics, 1997

Taylor, Frederick Winslow, *The Principles of Scientific Management*, New York, NY, USA and London, UK: Harper & Brothers, 1911

Tupper, H and Ellis, S, *The Squiggly Career, Ditch the Ladder, Discover Opportunity, Design Your Career,* Penguin Books, 2020

Wallace, Christina, *The Portfolio Life: Future-Proof Your Career and Craft a Life Worthy of You,* Ebury Edge, 2024

Whillans, Ashley, *Time Smart: How to Reclaim Your Time and Live a Happier Life* The Harvard Business Review Press, 2020

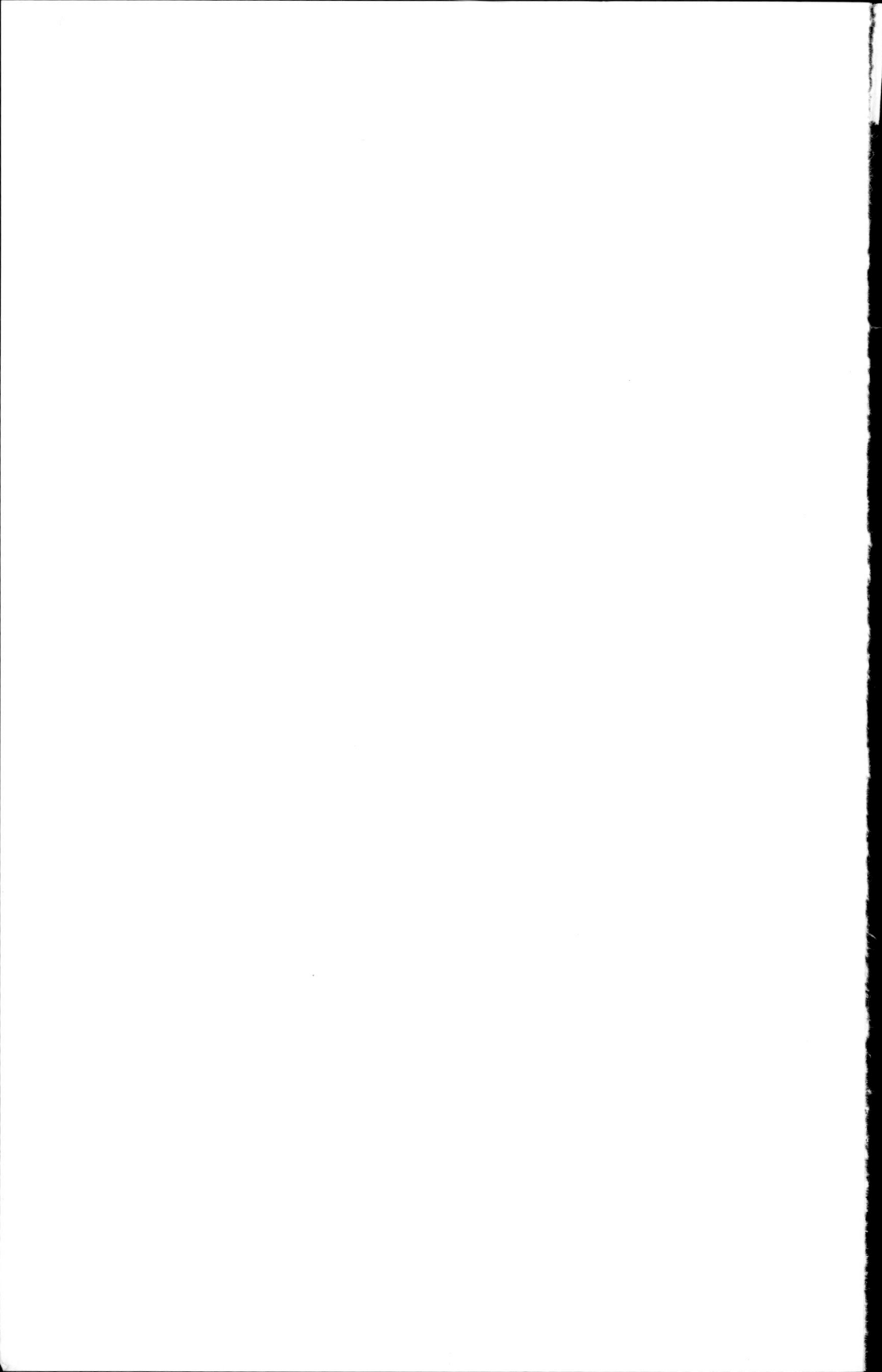